The Judgment by Michelangelo

VICI VINDICIAE: The Vindication of Giambattista Vico

Giorgio A Pinton

VICI VINDICIAE: The Vindication of Giambattista Vico

Nature, machine-like, works definitely and heartlessly, if in the main beautifully. Hence if we, as individuals, do not make this dream of a God or what he stands for to us, real, in our thoughts and deeds—then He is not real to us.

—Dreiser (1934)

TABLE OF CONTENTS

Part Three

PREFACE

The Vici Vindiciae of *Donald Phillip Verene*

In the journal *New Vico Studies* (Vol. 24, 2006), Professor Donald Phillip Verene—I will make sure that you will get the correct information—translated, commented, and published "Vico's Reply to the False Book Notice: The *Vici Vindiciae.*" He composed the article in four parts. First, Verene introduced what caused the anger of Vico and the writing of his vindication against the misinformation given by editors of the *Acta* in their book-review of the *New Science* of 1725. The book, wrote Verene, "had not been received by the Italians with the tedium claimed in Leipzig book notice, but by Vico's own assessment it was also not received with applause." Some dear friends of Vico, however, praised him enough to the point that Vico main work after 1725 until his death continued to be the problems of the true nature and content of the *New Science*. Names like Father Bernardo Maria Giacco, a Capuchin; Abbé Luigi Esperti; Father Edouard de Vitry, a French Jesuit; Francesco Saverion Estevan, a lawyer; are always mentioned as individuals who read the *New Science* as you read a Pulitzer Award Book. Their adoration for Vico was blinding. No wonder we hear more often, even today, people who criticize him than people who say that truly they understand him. Thus imagine this. Our Vico, after all the efforts he employed to make his book acceptable to the printer, having to reduce it from approximately 500 pages to more or less 250 and making it economically affordable to himself; having to help in the publicizing and marketing of the more or less 1,000 copies printed; having had negative local criticism from G. F. Finetti; how do you think he was feeling in his 26 years (1699-1725) already spent as professor at the University of Naples? The copy for the *Acta* editor was personally brought to LeClerc or Mencken the beginning of 1726 by the servant of a friend of Vico, as he did for the *De Uno* a few years before. Can anyone believe it? He already had given up the hope

9

of hearing from the *Acta* probably when actually the *Acta* had already appeared in August 1727 in Europe. Vico, in 1728, was working on his autobiography and on illustrations and comments on the new *New Science*, the one of 1730. In Naples, only in the summer of 1729, the voice circulated about a book of Vico being reviewed in the *Acta*, as one copy of it was read in a Naples's bookstore, not far from where Vico resided. Vico bought it and kept it. What joy and pain simultaneously and gradually pervaded the reader! In this light, we should read the vindication of our unfortunately most often forgotten Neapolitan Vico. In the same year, against the same book of which he just came to know the recension of the *Acta*, on 19 October, an ecclesiastical censure was pronounced by Giovanni Rossi, the member of the Neapolitan Holy Office. It was one disaster after another, and Vico for this censure had to withdraw the so much hoped Venetian edition from being printed.

The second part of Verene's article touches the problem of the identification of the one individual who gave malevolent information to the editors of the *Acta*. Who was the *Ignotus Erro*? "The great mystery of the false book notice is: who wrote it and sent it to the *Acta*?—wrote Verene—Who is the Italian friend whom Vico refers to as the unknown vagabond"? Pietro Giannone, published the *Civil History of the Kingdom of Naples* in 1723 (translated into English in London in 1729-1731) and in it he reconsiders the papacy self-serving claims about divine law and to raise the question of what it meant to be a Neapolitan and what it meant to be a Catholic. The work gave the right impression of being opposed to the Counter Reformation and was condemned. So did the *New Science* of Vico as interpreted by G.F. Finetti but on the contrary the *New Sience* was tolerated because of the methodology of fogginess used by its author and the absurd declarations of a terminology of faith whose deep meaning escaped to friendly Ecclesiastic reviewers of the work. Gustavo Costa said—Verene's quote—"The New Science should be viewed as a Trojan Horse, full of forbidden ideas having the potential to destroy the Counter-Reformation system, which were unwittingly allowed to enter the citadel of the old regime." In trying to find an answer to the question presented in this second part, Verene introduces an enigmatic, little studied, often mentioned colleague of Vico and also known as his tormentor who used to call Vico with unflattering epithets. Nicola Capasso was the approving secular reviewer of Giannone's work, a collaborator of the *Acta*, a teacher of law who held a different idea of the natural law than that of Vico. Another person should enter the scene. Verene speaks of two friends, the Abbe Giovanni Acampora and Carlo Giannone, Pietro's brother, who must have share the information that Pietro Giannone on 13 June 1728 wrote, saying that Acampora would have been sickened on knowing that the compilers of the *Acta* had great difficulty in understanding the fantastic and unfathomable ideas of Giambattista Vico. In addition he added, "in order to twist one's brain, it is only necessary to sniff his little book." From all this, yes, Giannone may very well be the culprit. Vico may have thought this, too. Giannone had suffered so much because of the long hand of the church, the empire, and the Savoy, that I do not, however, believe that he could have malevolently hit another Neapolitan.

The third part implicates Verene in explaining the title and the legal terminology. The *vindiciae* term appeared in the *Law of the Twelve Tables* (Table XII, 3) "in the context of adjudication of a false claim of ownership and it is an issue of civil law that involves the intervention of both parties. This direct involvement is vented by the expression of the Tables (VI. 5a-b) that Vico also uses (1. 39), *manum conserere* (to join hand in combat), a traditional resolution of a dispute by a trial by battle by our ancients. Verene completes this part identifying and explaining the meaning and use of *vindico*, *vindicatio* with the English vindicate. This elaborated part of the essay is very important under the legal implications that Vico must have considered and expressed in writing the text in light of his legal mind, expertise, studies, and various purposes for which he indeed wrote such a defense, which actually never sent to the editors of the *Acta*. He published it in Naples for Naples, for the government of Naples, and the citizens of Naples.

For the last part on rhetorical principles and motive of Vico's defense, we will only give the introductive paragraph of Verene.

> Vico's defense is based on four main tactical principles: repetition of the opponent's errors of fact; attribution to the opponent of the same form of thought the opponent has criticized; employment of the same manner of speech in addressing the opponent that the opponent has used; and affirmation of the most sensitive critical claim made by the opponent, not as a defect, but as a great truth of the case.

Part One

A LOOK AT GIAMBATTISTA VICO

Vico's Vision

Vico had his own vision of man and the universe, and, in a time when the deductive method brought into fashion by Descartes was much employed, he posed the modern problem of sense: the sense of life and of history. He discovered the irrational, the small flame that at certain times grows imperceptibly in the heart of reason. His philosophy recognized the aspirations of humanity, its obsessions and dreams, its precarious achievements, and its frustrations and defeats. He described human societies as passing through stages of growth and decay. The first is a "bestial" condition, from which emerges "the age of the gods," in which man is ruled by fear of the supernatural. "The age of heroes" is the consequence of alliances formed by family leaders to protect against internal dissent and external attack; in this stage, society is rigidly divided into patricians and plebeians. "The age of men" follows, as the result of class conflict in which the plebeians achieve equal rights, but this stage encounters the problems of corruption, dissolution, and a possible reversion to primitive barbarism. Vico affirmed that Providence must right the course of history so that men can be held within the right orders to practice justice as members of the society, of the family, of the state, and finally of mankind. Unable to attain all the utilities he wishes, he is constrained by these orders to seek those which are his due; and this is called just.

Early Life And Career

Vico was the son of a poor bookseller. In his family's home everyone was miserably huddled together in a mud-floored, ground-level room used simultaneously as a bookshop, living room, and kitchen. When he was scarcely seven, Vico injured his head falling from the ladder that led to the small second-floor attic that served as the sleeping room. The injury appeared so serious that the doctor predicted that it would lead to death or imbecility. Although the injury healed, he became stern and melancholic in nature. Vico later acknowledged this in his autobiography and observed: "such a nature do men with profound and active spirits possess."

He attended various schools, including a Jesuit college, for short periods but was largely self-taught. He had to study by candlelight in a miserable room crowded with a large family. He often skipped his classes, because his mediocre teachers could offer him nothing more than an arid Scholasticism, the system of Western Christian philosophy that flourished from the 11th to the 15th century but had declined greatly by the time of Vico. Despite his life of poverty, he was able to escape occasionally to the countryside; these excursions opened immense horizons beyond his limited early environment. In fact, personal experience, rather than reading, was the primary source of Vico's unique genius, although his reading was extensive, varied, and always distinguished by a personal interpretation.

In the course of his reading Vico encountered his first master, the Greek philosopher Plato. A critical spirit quickly intervened, and he turned to Tacitus, a Roman historian, and to Machiavelli, an Italian statesman and political philosopher, who portrayed men not as they should be but as they unfortunately are. Thus, contrasts soon became an important element in his thought: between nature and spirit; between the body, as "this somber prison," and the soul; between the high aspirations of the imprisoned soul and the fall that awaits it when it yields to the desires of the senses.

Vico's thought became increasingly independent, and he preferred to meditate in solitude; but, at the same time, he frequented the fashionable salons, where he met several scholars of the time, such as Thomas Corneille, a French dramatist, and Giovanni Mario Crescimbeni, a literary historian, with whom he debated. Gradually, this circle of scholars became attracted by the ideas of René Descartes, Benedict de Spinoza, and John Locke, which were penetrating Naples at the end of the 17th century. Although Vico was distantly involved in the controversies, he continued to depend more upon the course of his own self-instruction.

Following an attack of typhus, Vico left Naples and accepted a tutoring position in the home of the Duca della Rocca at Vatolla, south of Salerno, where he wrote his most authentic, and most despondent, poetry. There, secretly infatuated with his pupil, the young Giulia della Rocca, he discovered the pain of "social barriers"—barriers that were insuperable, because they were the vestige of entrenched ancient structures. Giulia, who admired Vico, died at the age of 22, shortly after her marriage to a young man "of her sphere." Although Vico always had a longing for a peaceful world, he felt that the discord that governs the individual spreads and that history itself only partially obeys the designs of Providence.

After his return to Naples, Vico found the next few years less difficult. He recovered from his ill-fated passion and in December 1699 married a childhood friend, Teresa Destito, who was well intentioned but almost illiterate and incapable of understanding him. In the same year, he obtained a chair of rhetoric at the University of Naples. One of the duties of the professor of rhetoric was to open the academic year with a Latin oration, and Vico carried out this responsibility by giving the introductory lectures between 1699 and 1708. The last one, printed in 1709 under the title *De Nostri Temporis Studiorum Ratione* ("On the Method of the Studies of Our Time"), is rich with his reflections about pedagogical methods. This work was followed almost immediately by the publication of Vico's great metaphysical essay *De Antiquissima Italorum Sapientia* ("On the Ancient Wisdom of the Italians"), which was a refutation of the Rationalistic system of Descartes.

This tranquil interval, during which he brought his aging father to live with him, did not last. Three of his eight children died at an early age, and another, Ignazio, caused his parents grave anxiety and was even imprisoned for his debts. Vico was also disappointed in his own career, which had initially appeared promising. He failed to obtain the more prestigious and better paid chair of law that he actively sought. When a notice contemptuous of his work appeared in one of the scholarly publications, his fiery temper was sparked, and he wrote his pamphlet "Vici Vindiciae" ("The Vindications of Vico") in reply. It was distressing for him to see so many mediocre thinkers favored and to be unable to ensure publication of his most important work.

1. FOR THE STUDY OF THE NEW SCIENCE

Leon Pompa, *Vico: A Study of the New Science* (Cambridge University Press, 1990) Professor Pompa's study of Vico has done a great deal to stimulate and inform the growing interest in the English-speaking world in this remarkable figure. It remains the only work devoted almost exclusively to an interpretation of the *New Science* and offers a comprehensive guide to the main theoretical problems to which the text gives rise. For this second edition Professor Pompa has responded to the reactions of reviewers and critics and added a new chapter which analyses Vico's conception of the principles which govern the development of law.

Reviewed by Robert Miner, Baylor University

Composed in 1725 but never before published in a full-length English edition, *The First New Science* is Leon Pompa's translation of the first version of the master work that Vico wrote and rewrote until his death in 1744. Understandably, the editors of the series in which this serviceable translation appears (Cambridge Texts in the History of Political Thought) decided not to go with the text's full title. *Principles of a New Science Concerning the Nature of the Nations, Through Which the Principles of a New System of the Natural Law of the Gentes are Retrieved* does not fit very well on a book's front cover.

A small number of Vico connoisseurs have persistently claimed that the 1725 version of the *Scienza nuova*—dubbed the *Scienza nuova prima* by Vico himself in his *Autobiography*—is a more readable text, and a more illuminating guide to its author's intentions, than the better known 1744 edition. Some who have made this claim also allege that Vico wrote the final *Scienza nuova* when he was senile—although it might be remembered that at least one of his contemporaries claimed that Vico was mad as far back as 1720. These speculations aside, the suggestion that the 1725 *Scienza nuova* is a less cluttered text than either the 1730 or 1744 versions is not implausible. The *Scienza nuova prima* is divided into five books. Book 1, "The Necessity of the End and the Difficulty of the Means of Retrieving a New Science," begins with a relatively clear statement of the problem. Neither philosophers nor philologists have adequately discerned the origins of human culture. Books 2 and 3 perform the work of retrieval, unearthing respectively the "Principles of This Science Through Ideas" and the "Principles of This Science From the Side of Languages." Book 4 provides the "Ground of the Proofs Which Establish This Science," and Book 5 narrates the "Development of the Matter Whence a Philosophy of Humanity and a Universal History of the Nations are Formed at the Same Time." The titles may be cumbersome, but they are relatively descriptive. Vico's decision to provide each Book with its own Latin motto (taken from Virgil, the poets, the Latin heralds, the philosophers, and the historians) adds a touch of elegance, and even clarity.

Long before it became fashionable, Vico relentlessly criticized philosophers who suppose rational discourse to owe little or nothing to the pre-rational discourses of myth, law, and poetry. In our own time, some philosophers schooled in the Anglo-American tradition of the last century have grown skeptical about the value of "pure" conceptual analysis divorced from historical reality. One notable example of this phenomenon is Bernard Williams. Williams characterizes the approach of Nietzsche, which he increasingly finds congenial, as one that "typically combines, in a way that analytical philosophy finds embarrassing, history, phenomenology, 'realistic' psychology, and conceptual interpretation" (Williams, *Making Sense of Humanity*, pp. 75-6). Something similar is true of Vico. Anti-historical philosophy and anti-philosophical philology have both failed, Vico announces in the *First New Science*, because "we have hitherto lacked a science that is both a history and philosophy of humanity" (p. 18, §23). Vico may be regarded as the father of all modern attempts, from Williams and Alasdair MacIntyre to Collingwood and Hegel, to effect a rapprochement between

18

history and philosophy. He is also the ancestor of contemporary attempts to recover a positive conception of rhetoric against the strictures of 'method,' as the opening pages of Gadamer's *Truth and Method*, which explicitly invoke Vico, would suggest.

It would not be impossible for an Anglophone reader to draw these conclusions by reading *The New Science of Giambattista Vico*, the generally excellent and widely available translation of the 1744 *Scienza nuova* by Thomas Goddard Bergin and Max Fisch. Such a reader would also be well served by David Marsh's recent translation of the same text. But her task will be made considerably easier by the availability of an English edition of the 1725 version. As such, both Pompa and the editors of the Cambridge Texts in the History of Political Thought are to be commended.

2. THE DISTRIBUTION OF PERSONALIZED COPIES
by Vico and G. L. Esperti

The book in itself is like an unexploded Hiroshima rocket falling on the heart of the 18th century. Instead of being a noticeable explosion, the book activates its energy with the passing of time. It will change the essential aspects of all the European nations and move them toward an equality of common developments that would bring each to emerge in their own way. Nobody knows exactly by whose mind it came to be. Its author is announced with a lot of malevolent misinformation. The author reacts controlling his anger, making it purely visible in a rhetorical process, correcting the information and returning to its being a member of the Neapolitan high society, while belonging to the learned one, without directly sending its vindication to the Leipzig Scholars. Vico knew that the effects of his rocket will activate with the passing of time. Croce himself uses the terms "bomba" and "explosion" in his narration of the events pertaining the *New Science* and the *Vici Vindiciae*.

In the third chapter of the first volume of the *Bibliografia Vichiana*, (pp. 34-41) Benedetto Croce narrated the birth in 1725 of the *New Science*, how Vico personally paid for its printing, and how he did its marketing. Perhaps, more than a marketing, as it did for the *Universal Right*, it was a distribution of many copies out of 1012 printed to friends, disciples, admirers, and prestigious literati, all Neapolitans, members of the clergy or of government or in highest positions. Croce lists all the documented distribution of copies (one or more, for those who at their own turn could bring copies to friends etc. outside Naples city and Kingdom).

Copies ms. of the unreduced *New Science* in forma negativa were given to Lorenzo Corsini (1653-1740), Pope starting in 1730, to whom the book is dedicated, though he never helped the author with the printing expenses. Then, Filippo Maria Monti (1675-1754) of Bologna, Francesco Buonocore of Ischia, and Padre Lodoli received a copy of it and when he returned it to Vico for the failure of the Venetian Edition

Vico gave it to Francesco Solla. But without the support, he reduced the book in forma negativa to 250 pages for which he paid. The Imprimatur was given on 18 October 1725.

The printing was to be of 1012 copies, perhaps partially ready by 25 October 1725, when one copy was given to

Bernardo Maria Giacco of Arienzo (1672-1744);

Francesco Rocca (1672-1740) Marquis of Vatolla;

Giuseppe Luigi Esperti of Rome received several copies with
> autograph dedications in each one, for distribution to
>> Celestino Galiani (1728-1787);
>> Eduard De Vitry, Jesuit;
>> Giambattista Salerno (1670-1729), Jesuit, Cardinal;
>> Ludovico Sergardi (1670-1726) [Quinto Settano], Cleric;
>> Francesco Bianchini and to unknown others;

Vico used again Esperti for this sort of distribution of his work:
> Lorenzo Corsini (1652-1740), who gave it to Alessandro Gregorio Capponi (1683-1746)

In January of 1726 Esperti received another box with various copies for
> Alvaro Cienfuegos, Cardinal (1657-1739), ambassador;
> Melchiorre of Polignac (1661-1741), ambassador;
> Luigi Pico della Mirandola (1669-1743), Cardinal;
> Giannantonio Davia of Bologna (1660-1740), Cardinal;

Esperti received again three copies in Venice for
> Antonio Schinella Conti (1677-1749);
> Francesco Carlo Lodoli (1690-1761);
> Gian Artico di Porcia (1682-1743);

Giuseppe Athias (1672-1745), in Livorno, received 5 (Croce, *B.V.*, I, p. 39): one for himself and one for each of the following gentlemen:
> Giuseppe Averani of Pisa (1662-1738);
> Anton Maria Salvini of Florence (1653-1729);
> Jean LeClerc, Amsterdam (1657-1727/1736?); last book is of 1724;
> Isaac Newton in London (1642-1726/1727);

Johann Burckard Mencken (1674-1732) in Leipzig (supposition that Acampora or Capasso bought copy from Felice Mosca and sent to the *Acta*) or through Neapolitan scholars teaching abroad, as it is the case of the son of Giuseppe Valletta (1636-1714), professor at the State University of Sweden. It should be possible to verify whether there still a copy exists at the library of the *Acta* and see whether it has any dedication to Le Clerc or Mencken.

These exemplars coming directly from Vico have all some dedicatory lines on the title page and some marginal or interlinear autograph additions or corrections. Three of my articles on the modifications made by Vico on the copies of particularly the De Uno (*Universal Right*) explain why and how Vico personalized the free copies distributed. Croce described also how the same personalization was made by Vico for copies distributed of the *New Science*. (See *Bibliografia Vichiana*, vol. 1, pp. 34-41.)

The next brief note concerns the *De Uno*, the previous book Vico sent into Europe for evaluation by Le Clerc in his journals.

3. HOW VICO MARKETED HIS OWN BOOKS

The Prince Wildenstein is mentioned once in the *Autobiography* (p. 159), once in *Vico, Opere* by Battistini (p. 1290); in both, Wildenstein is not in the index. Croce is more generous and in the *Bibliografia Vichiana* (vol. 1, pp. 24-25) gives us more information on the book and on some special exemplars produced on better paper and larger dimensions that are in part valid for the exemplar under our consideration:

> In conformity with what he promised in the *Synopsis*, between the end of August and the beginning of September 1720 Vico published the work with the title "Joh. Baptistae Vici, *De uno universi iuris principio et fine uno liber unus, ad amplissimum virum Franciscum Venturam, a Regis consiliis et criminum quaestorem alterum* (Excudebat Neapoli Felix Musca ex publica auctoritate, MDCCXX)." In almost all other published works, previously and afterward, Vico—faithful even in the physical aspects of things to the maxim that true scholars should publish books that are small but full of their own thoughts (*Opere*, vol. 1, 215)—adopted and will adopt the agile cut of the *dodicesimo*. On the contrary, the *De uno* as well as the *De Constantia* and the *Notae*, were printed in *quarto*. Thus, the *De Uno* was apt to contain the all matter in 195 numbered pages, plus four unnumbered in the beginning, dedicated to the frontispiece, the epigraph from Cicero, and to the reviews for the permission to print. How many exemplars were printed on common paper, it is not known; perhaps, one thousand as for the *Scienza nuova prima*. We are instead certain that several ones were printed on paper distinguished by remarkably wide margins. Of these exemplars, between October or November 1720, one was sent, by the courtesy of the Neapoletanized Florentine Alessandro Rinuccini (1686-1758), to Anton Maria Salvini (see *Opere*, vol. 5, p. 156); a second, ..., was sent later on, together with the *De constantia*, to Prince Eugene of Savoy; a third one, at last, for the suggestion of the Domenican Neapolitan erudite Tommaso Maria Alfano ... was trusted, on 9 February 1722 and also this time together with the *De constantia,* in the hand of the young Count of Wildenstein, in order that he would, once arrived at Louvain, bring both volumes to Jean LeClerc (see *Opere*, vol. 5, p. 177).

But, about Wildenstein, Croce says only that he was a young aristocrat, disposed to do Vico a favor. Fausto Nicolini, in Giambattista Vico, *Opere* (Riccardo Ricciardi Editore: Milano-Napoli, 1953), seems to have some extra information beside those we already have heard. In the note, at p. 113, he says that the name Wildenstein can be read as Wallenstein or Waldstein; that our Wildenstein was the descendant from the famous warrior (Albrecht von Waldstein–Wallenstein, 1583-1634) and the ascendant of Francis Adam von Waldstein (1759-1823), the future protector and benefactor of Giacomo Casanova. How Nicolini was able to collect this information, and from where or whom we could not find. Thus, unfortunately, besides Vico's mention of Wildenstein being in Naples, it appears that there are no others.

On 9 January 1722 writing to Le Clerc, Vico narrates about his connection with the Count of Wildenstein: "The Most Rev. Father Tommaso Alfano, our truly famous literato, who enjoys a continuous correspondence with you, gave me the excellent suggestion of humbly asking the services of the Count of Wildenstein, praying him that from Louvain, where he goes for his studies, he be so generous to bring you this work, so that what this work does not have in itself of worthiness it will have it from the dignity of the personage who carries it to your most esteemed person." The Count, however, had no interests in meeting LeClerc; it appears that he sent someone on his service to carry Vico's gift to Leclerc, as LeClerc on 8 September 1722 acknowledges in his letter to Vico. This is as much as we can say about the Count of Wildenstein and Vico, for the reason that Vico never mentioned that he gave an extra copy with the copy of the work he was supposed to bring to someone else, by the duty of courtesy and thankfulness, I assume, also to the young noble going to continue the studies begun in Naples at the famous Catholic University of Louvain, founded in 1425 by Duke John IV.

For what we know, the young Count of Wildenstein became famous because he brought, first, a book of Vico to Jean LeClerc, the most famous literato in Europe; second, was mentioned in the correspondence between Vico and LeClerc; and third, Vico dedicated an exemplar of his work to him.

4. HOW VICO MADE CORSI AND RICORSI OF CHANGES TO HIS MAJOR WORKS

Records make public the existence and the characteristics of another exemplar of Giambattista Vico's *De universi juris uno principio et fine uno* (DU) *and De constantia jurisprudentis* (DC), both works in a single volume, similarly to the volume Vico donated to F. F. A. Gervasi, in 1734. In addition, the essay asks whether the project's program and suggestions of Vincenzo Placella for the definitive edition of the *Diritto Universale*—DU, DC, and Notae (N) combined—is feasible.

Vincenzo Placella, in "Alcune Proposte per la Nuova Edizione delle Opere di Vico," in *Bollettino del Centro di Studi Vichiani* (VIII, 1978), and Fabrizio Lomonaco, in Giambattista Vico, *De Universi Juris Uno Principio et Fine Uno* (Liguori Editore: Napoli, 2007), have spoken of three exemplars, identifiable by the name of the city's library that owns them, or the name of the city where they are preserved, or the name of the person for whom Vico wrote the dedication, or the signature assigned to them by the librarians. The experts know the particular characteristics of these three exemplars. By presenting these characteristics, we will arrive to the main issue of our interest.

Placella speaks of the exemplar of the Biblioteca Casanatense of Rome, where the volume arrived for Tommaso M. Minorelli, the curator, sometime during the first two weeks of September 1721, and this exemplar goes under the signature H XIII 13 (also given as H XIII 12, in Placella, p. 79). In 2009, to an inquiry about it, using the signature H XIII 13, the librarian for the "Fondo Manoscritti e Opere Rare" of the Biblioteca Casanatense replied that in the register of the concordances the signature H XIII 13 was inexistent. This exemplar was intended for a public readership and not for a single reader, and this explains why it is said to possess margins cleared of the author's interventions, with only one noticeable comment in calce, and accurate and clean direct corrections of small printing errors or of linguistic nature of the text DC are, contrary to what can be found in the previous exemplar, enriched with numerous autograph interventions of the author, from simple corrections of words to the addition of complete short essays that fit between the margins. We know about the comments in this exemplar and of many others because Vico, on the suggestion of Prince Giambattista Filomarino, at last decided to print a book full only with comments, rectifications, substitutions, and additions. Filomarino must have paid for that. The trilogy of *Diritto universale* was thus completed with the third book, the Notae (N), which received its final approval for publishing on 13 August 1722.

Given that all of our discourse verges on the autograph presence (personally produced by Vico) of ink marks or spots, symbols, legible or illegible compositions of alphabetic letters within the printed text and its wide right/left and top/bottom margins, we may ask about the method Vico used to preserve the copy of these profusely added marginal observations and comments, as we find them printed in N. Placella answers by describing the third surviving exemplar copy that binds together DU, DC, and N.

This third exemplar is a volume of 580 pages that contains all the three books we mentioned, and includes four separate printed sheets of the *Sinopsi*, which is a condensed summary of the DU, in a journalistic style and typing; a letter dated 13 September 1722 of Biagio Garofalo; and a nine pages handwritten list of the printer's errors in the first two books, with suggested corrections (*Mendorum ab typis literariis Emendationes*). Garofano's letter and some observations on its date, with more information on DU, can be read in "Regarding the De Uno ..." in *New Vico Studies* 26 (2008). In that article, the names of the translators ad of the publishers of the translations of the DU, DC, and N are mentioned.

Vico kept this volume for his own use and consultation until 1734 when, having completed the most famous work of the *New Science* and reached the age of 66, he gave it to F. F. A. Gervasi, of whom we still know nothing. From Gervasi or his estate, through the different ownership of Giuseppe Solari and Filippo Raffaelli, this volume ended at the Biblioteca Nazionale of Naples, where it received the signature XIII B 62, which seems the one still valid. Placella considers this volume the unique tool for the understanding of the mental evolution and methodology Vico used throughout his professional career. The abundance of autograph material contained in the first two books, will allow the clarification of the stratification of Vico's corrections and comments. The third book *Notae* is also certainly very important for the study of the edoctica and the stratification of material: N (p. 79, lines 29-34) is the only one of the three books in which Vico cancelled completely a sentence in a manner that it is illegible and substituted it with another one he wrote in the margin. The number of the people that received N was limited. Every copy of DU and or DU-DC donated or sold before the end of September-October 1722 required Vico's attention, reflection, great patience, knowledge of persons and their interests; expertise, tremendous efforts, time, and rest when too sharp the pain due to his rheumatoid arthritis; ink supply, feather pens, and absorbent paper; visual memory of the material, and decision making on which single error to correct or which comment to add in calce, in a clean, neat, accurate, legible way, without maculating the page, as he did in the copy he kept for his own use (Gervasi Codex).

Having Vico preserved for a while and then printed in *Notae* the extensive autograph comments added to in separate sheets or written on the margin of the copy sent to Prince Eugene, the Naples codex became enormously rich of all kinds of manifestations of the working mind of Vico, of the stratifications of thought and its fossilizing into words that are unchangeable once printed in the final page. Vico had to use the Gervasi Codex as his guide to hunt for editorial imperfections, which are almost countless so that it would be almost impossible to correct their entirety, in a single session. The solution Vico decided for was to adopt this task: correct, add, change the printed text not as the text needed, but as the receiver would look at it. The Gervasi Codex remaining the original source from which to copy the selected comments; not all, and not at random, but according to the intellectual level or knowledge of the subject of the person to whom he intended to give the books as a gift. Before the opportunity of studying the Wildenstein Codex, I considered the Gervasi Codex the Ur-copy of all existing copies of DU, DC, and N, known or still unknown. After September 1722, however, what reason could Vico have to adorn with any comment future copies to be given in gift? Would the discovery of any new exemplar add anything to our already acquired knowledge of Vico's mental functionality, technological ability, and psychological interperspective selectivity of readers of his own works? Placella says, "The stratifications within the corpus of autograph apostils are … evident, even if we only pay attention to the ink and the ductus"; and Francesco Predari's edition of the Diritto universale also underlines the importance of stratigraphic problems of additions and rectification of thought performed by Vico in his writings on the margins of each copy.

Beside the mss. of the *De Uno* in Naples and Vienna, how many other copies of the *De Uno* are known as being rich in Vichian of these works, "which could give an image of the chronological and progressive order with which ideas became alive in the thought of Vico."

The Ur-codex must be the richest codex for showing the largest number of autograph corrections made of printing-errors, some of which are listed in the autograph Mendorum … Emendationes document, and repeated partly in Insigniora Priorum duum Librorum Menda Emendata at page six of the unnumbered pages of the introduction to N (Vico's letter to Giambattista Filomarino). In the Ur-codex margins, the most numerous autograph comments exist, which were included in N together with those written in the Vienna codex. We can safely state that no individual who received the two books, DU and DC, in one volume or only one of the two before 13 August 1722, received also the third (N). Why? Because, after September 1722, any sale or complimentary or gift copy of this work would have been of one single volume containing all three books (DU, DC, ad N). This assumption can very well explain why no surviving exemplar of a complete codex has been found, with the understandable exception of the Ur-codex in the private possession of the author. Consequently, the most valuable and interesting codices of these works for the people interested in Vico studies would be those given freely or sold after the autumn of 1720 for DU, and after the autumn of 1721 for the DU and DC, in one volume. Those given or sold after the fall of 1722 including DU, DC, and N, all in one volume, needed very little personal and demanding intervention of Vico, beside the personalization of the volume with an autograph dedication.

After the publication of the *Diritto Universale*, Vico still could, if he wanted, when giving copies of the volume (with the three books) out, correct the errors of grammar, syntax, and spelling that for many reasons were also due to Felix Musca. We will be very fortunate, if we could find one of these copies. Vico corrected only a part of all the errors of this kind that can be found in these three books and we have listed them in our Tables A and B. Furthermore, he did not keep record in DU, DC, and N of the Gervasi Codex of having done several other corrections that he simply listed in N, in the sixth unnumbered page, *Insigniora Priorum duum Librorum menda emendata*. Another list of printing errors, the *Mendorum ab Typis Literariis Emendationes*, in nine single sheets that he kept within the Gervasi Exemplar is certainly prior in time and importance to the printed one in N; it lists the Insigniora with several others that, too, have not been corrected by Vico in his copy. Vico left that job for his readers and us! Placella knew of no other exemplars and did not mention the possibility of finding any in the future. This is why we are urged to introduce known contemporary surviving exemplars of these works of Vico.

5. VICO'S APOSTILS

The apostils? What about the issue of when they were given out by Vico, in order for us to identify the most recent and most relevant one? Can anyone state until when Vico retouched the *XIII B 62* before giving it away in 1734, beside the sentence for the disciple that he wrote at the bottom of the title page? If no other copy exists with autographed apostils, then Nicolini edition would remain the most reliable edition, even with the few variations from *XIII B 62*. If even one more exemplar with apostils will become available, then the work of a definitive text of the *De Uno* that includes Vico's history of deletions, amends, variations, additions, in a word, the last words of Vico on the matter, will have to be postponed to the time when we will have found and studied all existent copies directly distributed by Vico; they seem all rich in apostils. This list will include, beside the two we are considering (F.F. A. Gervasi, and Eugene of Savoy), the copies of the *De Uno* sent to Luca Antonio Porzio (Rome, between August and September 1720), Bernardo Maria Giacco (Naples, 19 September 1720), Anton Maria Salvini (Florence, etymological and grammatical apostils, between October and November in 1720), Biagio Garofalo (Rome, 13 September 1721), Tommaso Maria Minorelli (Rome, 27 September 1721), and Jean Le Clerc (Louvain, 9 February 1722), Francesco Valletta (Uppsala, no date available), and Francesco Ventura, to whom the *De Uno* is dedicated. Of the approximate one thousand copies printed, these appear to be the ones we know about and that hopefully may be found. Then, if we could have a sequential inventory of all the autographed apostils of Vico that are contained in these copies, we could build a mirror of the growth and direction of the growth of Vico's mind, with textual criticism, ecdotics, and any other interpretive modern technique.

Biagio Garofalo, whom Vico mentioned in his notes to the *De Uno* as Blasius Caryophilus lived between 1677 and 1762, worked as an archaeologist for the Papal Court of Clement XI and then moved to

Vienna in order to be of service to the House of Prince Eugene of Savoy. Garofalo's research and publications, the like of *De Mercaturis Antiquorum* (Romae, 1718) and *De Antiquis auri, Argenti, Stanni, Aeris, Ferri, Plumbique Fodinis Opusculum* (Vienna, 1757), were of great interest and usefulness to the brilliant military strategist at the Court of the Habsburgs, which had often an empty Treasury. The *De Antiquis* is a rare treatise on minerals, metallurgy, and the exploitation of mines and constituted itself as the herald of the industrial growth in the nineteenth century. When in 1724 Biagio traveled to Vienna, he carried a special copy of each of the three volumes of what we know as *Diritto Universale*, all bound together, for Prince Eugene. The first volume, bounded with the second and third ones, is surviving in Vienna as exemplar "ms. B E VIII M 9," and Nicolini possessed a list of the inscriptions that Vico made on it.

On 11 September 1721, Pasquale Garofalo, a student of Vico and nephew of Biagio, arrived at Rome from Naples, carrying both tomes of the *Diritto Universale*, as a gift for his uncle. We can rest sure that both *De Uno* and *De Constantia* were given to Garofalo, because Vico in the above mentioned letter to Bernardo Maria Giacco, already on the 27 October 1721 could declare of having received confirmation and praises from Garofalo. Biagio's letter is in Italian and can be found not only as a copy of the autograph as part of "ms. De Uno XIII B 62," but also in Manuela Sanna, *Epistole* (n. 19).[1]

A pioneering treatise that aroused great controversy when it was first published in 1725, Vico's *New Science* is acknowledged today to be

---

[1] My three articles from which parts concerning the way Vico handled the distribution and marketing of copies of his work for friends or reviewers relate to the 3 volumes of the so called *Universal Right* or *Law* of the period 1721-1723 are: The "De Uno XIII B 62, the 'pastiche,' and the letters to or from Vico of Biagio Garofalo and Eugene of Savoy regarding the *De Uno*" in *New Vico Studies* vol. 26 (2008), pp. 103-125; the "The Maximiliam Wildenstein's *De Uno* and *De Constantia*" in *Bollettino del Centro di Studi Vichiani*, XL/2 (2/2010), pp. 127-188; the "Antonio Maria Salvini: I Marginalia al *De Universi juris principio uno et fine uno* di Giambattista Vico" in *Bollettino del Centro di Studi Vichiani*, XLIII (2013), pp. ???.

one of the few works of authentic genius in the history of social theory. It represents the most ambitious attempt before Comte at comprehensive science of human society and the most profound analysis of the class struggle prior to Marx.

In Vico's history of the emergence of thought, human consciousness begins with fear as a response to a loud noise, with thunder being a prime example as being perceived as the *Voice of God*. It is fear which makes the link between emotion and external stimulus that is at the bases of sensus communis, the 'common sense' known to all humanity. This is at the most archaic level of human understanding, based in the most original and primitive forms of speech as exclamatory yelps and shouts of emotion, within a layer of thought which is not logically derived and is non-rational like that of the animals.

Above this layer, is the layer of *topics*. *Topics* is the art of making the connecting logical link between two observable propositions. Poetic wisdom is the next layer above this, and it begins with a *theory of topics* as being the poetic formulae through which people identify the phenomena of the world. The link between two initial syllogisms, are self-coherent elements of thought. They provide fixed points of reference and a map upon which the flux of experience can be transposed and quantified.

These *puncta metaphysica* or 'metaphysical points' constituted a structure for the perception of reality, as the link between topics allowing for the connection to other links. They are points in memory, and could be likened to the stones and tidal pools left behind a crashing ocean wave (like raw experience) on a beach. As they multiply, the topics are abbreviated and are represented by metaphor: a particular image in the mind that is chosen to represent and remember a topic by.

Vico believed that the most ancient people thought in metaphor. As the knowledge of topics became more extensive, Vico understood metaphor as being continuously refined and transformed into three rhetorical figures befitting the three ages of civilizations: (1) *metonymy*, a vivid image of detail representing the complete expression of the topic, (2) *synecdoche*, an image that conveys just the character or 'look and feel' of a topic, (3) *irony*, were an image has acquired a meaning and a point of reference of its own, and has lost the connection between the originating topic. With irony, the process can start over, with new links between the newly isolated propositions. Vico's *new science* therefore is based in the conception of consciousness as a process of abstraction, which separates by forgetfulness, human thought from actual physical perceptions. It eventually places all human discourse adrift in a sea of ironic images, that are constantly and automatically refining and recompartmentalizing themselves into exhaustion as they approach the entropic heat death of a *recorso*, in this instance, a kind of cancer of the imagination.

Modern 18th century language and human discourse for Vico, had lost its connection with the imaginative poetic processes that originally formed it. Image and idea had become separated and unsynchronized. Vico foresaw the growth of the printed word, as increasing this separation by the profuse publication of 'unworthy' texts which no longer needed the vocal explanation of the rhetorician. Contact to the poetic code could be regained Vico believed by the historical reconstructions of the origins of language. History was therefore viewed by him and successors to his theories, as a set of images encoded upon the events of time, whose contemplation allowed one to recover forgotten and suppressed earlier forms of feral imaginative thinking. The quest for the origins of imaginative thought eventually became the primary goal of the Romantic poets and philosophers of the nineteenth century and was the heart of the early psychoanalytical theories of the twentieth century.

6. THE ACTA ERUDITORUM LIPSIENTIA
of the Month of August 1727
pp. 383-384

MENSIS AUGUSTI A.M D CC XXVII.　　383

tradictiones *philosophiæ naturalis*, circa continuitatem, homoge-
neitatem, gravitatem, divifibilitatem materiæ, per fuppofitionem
Immaterialismi, ceu nodum Gordium, uno ictu diffolvi, affirmat,
aliosque hujus doctrinæ ufus in *Moralibus, Metaphyficis & Ma-
thematicis* fubjungit. Atque ita Berkelejus paradoxon fuum de
non-exiftentia materiæ fpeciofe fatis defendit, de cujus veritate alii
judicent; de origine, quicquid Autor diffimulet, fic fentimus, ex
Cortefii, Malebranchii & Spinofa philofophiarum mixtura pro-
gnatum hoc λυβικὸν θηρίον. Cæterum ea, quam fub manibus ha-
bemus, horum Dialogorum editio altera eft; prior jam prodiit A.
1715, cujus amplam doctamque recenfionem Lector inveniet in
Diario Gallico *le Journal literaire Tom. I art. 16.*

NOVA LITTERARIA.

PRodiit Neapoli fuperiori anno vergente liber admodum elegans, cui titulus: *Camilli Eucherii de Quintiis, e Soc. Jefu, In-
crinue feu de Balneis Pithecufarum Libri VI, Sereniff. Lufitaniæ
Regi Joanni V dicati*, in 4 minori. Carmen eft heroicum, ad
Lucretii fere morem compofitum, notisque hiftoricis ac phyficis
eruditis illuftratum ac figuris aliquot belliffimis exornatum.
Prodiit & ibidem nuper liber fub tit. *Principi d'una nuova Scienza*, & Cujus libri Autor quamvis nomen fuum eruditos celet, certiores tamen facti fumus per amicum quendam Italum, effe eundem Abbatem Neapolitanum, cui nomen *Vici* fit. Agitavit Autor
in ifto libello novum Juris Naturæ Syftema aut figmentum potius,
ut alii longe, quam hactenus fueverunt Philofophi, principiis deductum, magisque ad ingenium Pontificiæ ecclefiæ accommodatum. Multo labore contra Grotii & Pufendorffii doctrinas &
principia difputat, ingenio tamen hic magis indulget quam veritati, longaque conjecturarum mole tandem fibi ipfi deficiens ab
pfis Italis tædio magis quam applaufu excipitur.

Genevæ Perachon & Cramer, Typographi, in duobus
Operibus, altero Juridico, altero Medico, recudendis valde
occupantur. Illa funt rara hactenus *Joannis del Caftillo Sotoma-
r* Opera, una cum *Jo. Pauli Melii* Additionibus & Obfervatio-
bus, & *N. Antonii* J. U. Doct. & Prof. Repertorio generali, X
　　　　　　　　　　　　　　　　　　　　Tomis

NOVA LITTERARIA * RECENT PUBLICATIONS

At p. 383, we have one first and the beginning of a second paragraph of the notice of the new literary works that appeared in some major cities of Europe in the previous one or two years.

The first paragraph announces the two books that have been published in Naples. In its first six lines the work honoring King John V of Lusitania (an area larger than present Portugal) in heroic verses is by Camillus Eucherius De Quintiis, a Jesuit, with the title *Inarime seu de Balneis Pithecusarum* Libri VI, printed by Felix Mosca (the same printer of Vico's work) in 1726. The second book announced is the *Principii d'una nuova Scienza* of Vico, in lines 7-17, that is, in the remaining part of the paragraph. Vico himself in the *Vindiciae* made known its content: see below *About the book and its review*, paragraph 2 (alphabet letters a-t).

The second paragraph makes known the two works, one on jurisprudence and another on medecine, that the typographers Perachon and Cramer of Geneva published. The law work is declared rare and its author is Joannis de Castillo Satomayor; it has the additions and observations of John Paul Melius and N. Anthony.

On p. 384, the first three lines refers the statements of the Sacred Roman Rota for the first time included in the work. Then, from the fourth line to the end of the paragraph, we have the notice on the medical works of Richard Morton, to which have been added the writings of Gualtherus Harris, Cole, Listerus, and Sydenham. This work, too, would hopefully come from the same printers of Geneva mentioned above. They are editing and inserting in the same work, the essays of Carol Leigh, the last ones of Gualtherus Harris, and the comments of Vincent Kattelaer on ... new methods of inoculation and vaccination.

The third paragraph concerns the intention of the famous London's printer Edmundus Chishull of publishing a series on Relics of Asiatic Antiquities (*Antiquitatum Asiaticarum Reliquiae*). The work would be in three parts, each one comprehending lists of new unedited artifacts from the Greek Asia Minor .... A clarifying description of the program intended by Chishull can be found, for those who wish, in Diarium Hagiense in *Histoire Literaire de l'Europe*, of June 1727, p. 180.

384 ACTA ERUD. M.AUGUSTI A. M.D CC.XXVII.

Tomis diſtributa, quæ ut nunc emendatiora & ad uſum magis accommodata, ita & ad calcem additionum Melianarum recentiſſimis S. Rotæ Romanæ Deciſionibus, hactenus ineditis, acta prodibunt. Hæc vero ſunt *Richardi Morton* Opera omnia, quæ jam olim una cum ſcriptis aliorum, *Gualtheri* nempe *Harris*, *Cole*, *Liſteri*, *Sydenham*, praxin pariter & materiam Medicam concernentibus, iidem Typographi ediderant, nunc aliis inſuper ſcriptis, *Caroli Leigh* Phthiſiologia Lancaſtrienſi, *Gualtheri Harris* ultimis Operibus, *Vinc. Kattelaer* M. D. Commentatio de Aphthis, & Diſſertationibus quorúndam de nova methodo inoculationis & transplantationis Variolarum aucta; quæ quidem Opera hoc ipſo anno proditura ſperamus.

Londini Cl. *Edmundus Chisbull* novum opus promiſit, publico programmate propoſito, quo inter alia hæc refert: *Titulum feret* : Antiquitatum Aſiaticarum Reliquiæ : *five nobiliores quædam ab Aſia Minore Inscriptiones Græcæ. Opus in tres Partes diviſum.* Prima *dabit Inscriptionum duarum Sigearum, cum commentario & notis, editionem novam. Accedent eidem Latina Monumenta duo : unum Ancyranum, ex autographis ſchedis Tournefortianis, longe quam antea auctius & emendatius : alterum Stratonicenſe, ex Itinerario Sherardiano nunc primum in lucem datum.* Secunda *complectetur Inscriptionum Græcarum ſeriem, numero circiter trecentarum, partem longe maximam hactenus ineditarum, a Teo, Lebedo, Epheſo, Mileto, Stratonicea, Magneſia ad Meandrum, Trallibus, Aphrodiſiade, Laodicea, Hierapoli, Philadelphia, Sardibus, Thyatiris, Pergamo, Lesbo Inſula, Smyrna, aliisque Urbibus Aſiaticis. Adjicientur paſſim breves nota criticæ, cum non paucis, de ſingulari quarundam Inscriptionum materia, & locis ubi reperta ſunt, Proæmiis.* Tertia *exhibebit Alphabeticum ad rariora & difficiliora Inscriptionum Commentarium; variosque, ſecundum methodum Scaligeranam & Reineſianam, Indices.* Ceterum quod ad ſpecimen, huic programmati ab Autore ſubjunctum, attinet, eo deſcribendo facile ſuperſedemus. Evolvant, qui legere cupiunt, Diarium Hagienſe *Hiſtoire Littéraire de l'Europe* M. Jun. 1727

p. 180.

Part Two

G. B. Vico by Carlo Rampoldi

The Vindication of Giambattista Vico

INTRODUCTION by G. A. Pinton

The intention of this work is to briefly introduce and offer a translation of the literary revenge that Vico took against the authors of a review of his *The First New Science* that is available in the English version of Leon Pompa with this same title.[2] Vico had sent a copy of the work to the director of the *Acta Eruditorum* of Leipzig, J. Burkhard Mencken, who examined it and furthermore asked information about its author from one of the journal's Italian correspondents. The review appeared anonymously in the August issue of the *Acta* of 1727 declaring that the author of *The First New Science* showed more ingenuity than truth in his exposition and that his theses were derived from uncommon philosophical principles, fully consonant with the teachings of the Roman Church, but polemical towards the theses of protestant scholars such as Grotius and Pufendorf. To Vico the anonymous review in Leipzig sounded like a reflection of positions that were held at least by some anti-curialists in Naples, who, even though receiving a copy of the work from him, did not acknowledge its reception. It appeared that his adversaries read him as a convinced supporter of Roman Christian doctrines, especially for his accentuation of the role of providence in human affairs. Vico's concept of providence, however, could not and should not be understood as the typical one professed by Catholicism. Vico holds that all religions have providence and that all human religious experiences

---

[2] Vico, *The First New Science*, Edited and Translated by Leon Pompa, Cambridge Texts in the History of Political Thought (Cambridge University Press, 2002). Even though this is today the commonly known title of this work, we may observe that Vico criticized the use of it in the review of the *Acta*. See *The Autobiography*, Translated from the Italian by Max Harold Fish and Thomas Goddard Bergin (Ithaca, N.Y.: Great Seal Books, 1963), p. 187: "The notice there given of it does not give the name of the book, which is the first duty of a reviewer, but calls it merely *New Science*, omitting [that part of the title which explains] the subject with which it deals."

themselves testify to a provident divinity, without which the religious phenomenon itself would be nonsensical.[3]

Vico's reaction to the Leipzig *Acta* in 1729, therefore, was soon to be interpreted as an intended reaction to adversaries abroad as well as at home and as a clarification of his own positions to himself and his readers. This justifies the exact title of the composition which is *Joh. Baptistae Vici Notae in Acta Eruditorum Lipsiensia* that means *Notes of Giambattista Vico on the Acts of the Erudites of Leipzig*. The writing of these pages took a few months (from August to October), but they are the expression of Vico's own pondering between 1727 and 1729. The letters to Bernardo Maria Giacco, Francesco Saverio Estevan [*see* them in *New Vico Studies*, vol. 19, 2001], and Ludovico Muratori, and the pages of the autobiography written during this time manifest precisely the continuous concern of Vico for a clarification of his thought and the way he should express it in language. Franco Ratto, in "Motivi di una rilettura delle *Vici Vindiciae*,"[4] reduced to two the points of criticism addressed to Vico by the scholars of Leipzig: the first point is on the definition or nature of *ingenium*; the second, on the definition and validity of the doctrine of providence. For him, the remarks of Vico are basically focusing on these same two points.

Ingenium (ingenuity, wit), Vico says in the 15th note, is interpreted by the critics of his system as *linguae genium* or rather as a special characteristic of the language that the Catholic church has adopted in disputations and argumentations and that proceeds according to preconceived assumptions with a disregard for truth. But this understanding of *ingenium*, we read in the 14th note, could be adopted by the Protestant church alone, either Lutheran or Calvinistic, which refuted throughout history the argumentations of the Church of Rome as

---

[3] A summary of the *Vici Vindiciae* is given by Vico in 1731 in the second part of *The Autobiography*, pp. 187–190. A copy of the letter Vico wrote but never sent to Mencken is also included.

[4] In *Percorsi della Ricerca Filosofica, Filosofie tra Storia Linguaggio e Politica* (Roma:Gangemi Editore, 1990), pp. 29–40.

arbitrary and done according to pre-established assumptions. The problem is that Leipzig academicians considered Vico as one who in his work dealt with figments of imagination, conjectures, and worthless stories.

Vico's rejection of this interpretation of his work is found in the 17th note where he declared to have spent thirty years of his life not in fantasies or figments of imagination but in a responsible, serious, and persevering scholarly research and reflection. In the 21st note, Vico moves from a defensive to an offensive position. He redefines the meaning of *ingenium* and shows that the concept of *ingenium* as contrastive to truth is absurd. The cleverness and originality of *ingenium* make it the divine author of all inventions and, among other examples Vico observes, the science of thinking based on this kind of *ingenium* is characteristic of the experimental philosophy practiced particularly by the English. The anonymous author of the review of *The First New Science* had formulated a second very serious accusation: the fictitious narrations in Vico's work are in contrast with the narrations of two most excellent philosophers, Grotius and Pufendorf. Vico had criticized Grotius for having affirmed that his system of laws could be valid even without assuming the existence of a divinity.[5] For Vico this was an impossibility

---

[5] See "Riprensione del sistema d'Ugone Grozio ne' libri *De iure belli et pacis*" in Fausto Nicolini, *Vico: Opere* (Bari: Laterza, 1942), vol. 4, pp. 253–254, pars. 1360–1362. In par. 1362, Vico says, "... it is now possible to understand that Grotius has written about the *right of war and peace* far less than half of what the subject deserved and without the science of its principles, contemplating all at once the nations already formed within the society of the whole humankind! This error originated from the other error of Grotius that consisted in his reasoning without considering those principles of divine providence that the Roman jurists themselves considered in their own reasoning. Divine providence first indoctrinated separately all nations, leaving each one without knowledge of others, about these universal laws. Afterward, when moving out of their own borders for motive of war, both the winning nation in dictating them and the conquered

since no man would join another man to form a society unless both assumed the existence of some kind of deity above them. In regard to Pufendorf Vico asserted that Pufendorf's Epicurean vision of a man inserted in a society without help and guidance of a divinity was also opposing his own theory of a providential deity.   Vico was not surprised by this charge for since the beginning of his reflection in a negative form, the first draft of *The First New Science*, he had formulated a system that was precisely and professedly contrary to the three great known philosophers, Grotius, Pufendorf, and Selden, who built systems that excluded the need of a providential deity. This was as much as he wrote to Filippo Maria Monti on October 1725. This intention was expressed in the dedication of *The First New Science* to Lorenzo Corsini, to which Vico dedicated the work. This was also the only part of the book that the Leipzig reviewer may have read.

Two observations may be made at this point. First, Vico sees providence as "the first principle of nations." Second, he admit that in the Church of Rome the teaching of this divine providence is mostly manifest and that he piously adhere to it. Thus, Vico admits the theoretical value of the principle of providence in the context of his work and states the conformity of such a principle with the doctrine of the Church of Rome. This, in Ratto's opinion, justifies the charges of the academicians of Leipzig. It is for this reason that Vico tries to confirm the correctness of his position by mentioning the philosophical tradition from Plato to Cicero, for whom providence was within the acknowledgment of all human beings, and by referring to the teaching of the Catholic church. This, too, according to Ratto, appears to give immediate legitimacy to the Leipzig accusations. The equanimous reader

---

one in receiving them, recognized them as just laws." Vico's criticism of the three political philsophers (Grotius, Pufendorf, and Selden) runs also through the first draft of *The First New Science* in the *Diritto Universale*, or *Universal Right*, Translated from Latin and Edited by Giorgio Pinton and Margaret Diehl (Editions Rodopi B.V., 2000).

of these reactions of Vico to the review in the *Acta* may formulate a different opinion after considering Vico's own words in the following text.

2. The Text

Thanks to the Consiglio Nazionale delle Ricerche and the Centro di Studi Vichiani, the 12th volume of the *Opere di Giambattista Vico*, titled *Varia, il De Mente Heroica e gli Scritti Latini Minori*, contains also the short work of Vico that goes under the name of *Vici Vindiciae.* Its full complete titles is *Joh. Baptistae Vici Notae in Acta Eruditorum Lipsiensia mensis Augusti a.MDCCXXVII ubi inter Nova Literaria Unum extat de eius libro cui titulus Principii d'una Scienza Nuova dintorno alla Natura delle Nazioni* (Notes of Giambattista Vico on the journal of the *Acts* of the Academicians of Leipzig of the Month of August 1927, in which among the reviews of new works there is one dedicated to his own work by the title *The Principles of a New Science of the Nature of Nations*). The curators of the text, Gian Galeazzo Visconti and Teodosio Armignacco, stated that the ms. runs through seventeen original notes identified with the letters of the alphabet from *a* to *q*, to which later two more were added, *r* and *s*, bringing the total of the original notes to nineteen. But in addition to the above, four more notes and three new variations were added to the original, which were identified by Vico with the letter *t*. Whatever the number of the extant mss. was and the identification of a final one adopted and brought to the printer by Vico, we solely rely on the work of the curators of the text collected in the 12th volume of Vico's *Opere*. It should be noticed that the present text is composed of a dedication and fifty-two paragraphs that are identified with Arabic numbers within brackets and include at times the alphabetic letters of Vico's unused subdivision.

3. The Translation

The work was published in Latin, but available is also the Italian version made by the curators of the original text. The expression "Vici Vindiciae" has been translated also as "in defense of Vico" in the translation of pars. 20—31 (letter *q*) of this work in *Forum Italicum,* 2 [1968], as "A Factual Digression on Human Genius, Sharp, Witty Remarks, and Laughter."

ARGUMENT & DEDICATION
of the *New Science* (1725)

The Dedication		
1. Vico's Vindication	2. To Charles of Austria	3. To Charles of Austria
G.B. Vico's Notes On the *Acta* of the Scholars of Leipzig of August 1727, where among other literary news there is one of his book whose title is *Principles of a New Science Concerning the Nature of Nations*	Roman Emperor and Pious and Felicitous King of the Spanish Lands Who as August Protector of the Roman-Catholic Religion in Italy has given rise through public instruction to the ingenuity of a Neapolitan citizen in such a way that he has meditated on a New Science about the Nature of Nations which demonstrates that the Natural Right of the People is properly suitable to such conditions of the civil societies having been born from them as the Truth. On this book, small in size but great for its subject matter, meditated in the spirit of such New Science Giambattista Vico Professor of Eloquence in the Royal University of Naples is submitting homage and	To Charles of Austria, Vico sends, gives and dedicates these glorious vindications in which though within the cultural limits of the book itself are defended the religiosity of the greatest Fatherland the dignity of the Italic Wisdom the truth of the Roman Catholic Church and the Majesty of Your Right as the Monarch against a hiding vagabond called to judgment before the Scholars of Leipzig as subpoenaed by the *Acta*

VICI VINDICIAE:

Vindication of Giambattista Vico, by Himself

VICI VINDICIAE

[1r] IOH. BAPTISTAE VICI

NOTAE

IN ACTA ERUDITORUM LIPSIENSIA

5   MENSIS AUGUSTI A. MDCCXXVII

UBI

INTER NOVA LITERARIA

UNUM EXTAT DE EIUS LIBRO CUI TITULUS

PRINCÍPI D'UNA SCIENZA NUOVA

10   DINTORNO

ALLA NATURA DELLE NAZIONI

CAROLO AUSTRIO

ROMANORUM IMPERATORI

ET HISPANIARUM REGI

PIO FELICI

5   QUI

ROMANO-CATH. RELIGIONIS

PROTECTOR AUGUSTUS

IN ITALIA

NEAPOLITANI CIVIS

10   INGENIUM

PUBLICA ERUDITIONE

EXCITAVIT

UT

NOVAM SCIENTIAM

15   DE NATIONUM NATURA

MEDITARETUR

QUAE

DE IURE

NATURALI GENTIUM

20   SYSTEMA

TALI POLITIA DIGNUM

AB IPSA NATUM

VERUM ESSE

DEMONSTRAT

25   IN HOC

MOLE QUIDEM PEREXIGUO

CAUSSA AUTEM

INGENTI LIBRO

PER OCCASIONEM

30   EIUS NOVAE SCIENTIAE

LUCUBRATO

UBI

QUASI IN MODICO SUO

DOCTRINAE FUNDO

35   ADVERSUS QUENDAM
APUD ACTA ERUDITORUM
LIPSIAE
LATITANTEM ERRONEM
MANU CONSERTUM
40   AMPLISSIMAE PATRIAE
PIETAS
ITALICAE SAPIENTIAE
DIGNITAS
ECCLESIAE ROMANO-CATHOL.
45   VERITAS
EIUSQUE MONARCHICI IURIS
MAIESTAS
VINDICANTUR
INCLYTAS VINDICIAS
50   IOH. BAPTISTA VICUS
IN EIUS REGIA ACADEMIA
ELOQUENTIAE PROFESSOR
IN OBSEQUIUM PROVOLUTUS
DAT DONAT DICATQUE.

THE *VICI VINDICIAE* or "The Legal Claim of Vico"[6]

THE DEDICATION

These notes of Giambattista Vico on the *Acta Eruditorum* of Leipzig of the month of August of 1727,[7] [within whose many new literary announcements one stands out with the title of *The Principles of a New Science of the Nature of Nations*] are dedicated to Charles of Austria, Emperor of the Romans and King of Spain, pious and privileged.[8] As

---

[6] As the good Romanist he was, Vico assigned this short title to the present writing making explicit its nature. The term *vindiciae* appears in the Twelve Tables with the general meaning of "laying claim to" something. This should explain the English title: "The Legal Claims of Vico" and the legal nature itself of these Vichian notes!

[7] Vico's legal claim vindicating his right to intellectual property and honorable name against the unknown slanderer is composed, as we saw in the introduction, of a precise number of observations, remarks, comments or notes, which are marked in the text with the letters of the alphabet (Vico) and bracketed numbers (introduced by the curators of the text). The English term "notes" does not truly translate the Latin *notae* used by Vico. We must insist on the legal nature of this work: like *vindiciae*, *notae* as well has its legal character. *Black's Legal Dictionary* defines *nota* as follows: "In the civil law, a mark or brand put upon a person by the law." Lewis and Short's *Latin Dictionary* explains, "*Nota censoria* or simply *nota*, the mark or note which the censors affixed in their lists of citizens in the name of any one whom they censured for immorality or want of patriotism." These are indeed the charges of Vico against the misrepresenter of his work.

[8] Charles VI of Austria (1685–1740), the son of Leopold I, whom Vico celebrated in his narration of the life of General Antonio Carafa, was the most admired sovereign Vico ever had. See Giambattista Vico, *Statecraft: The Deeds of Antonio Carafa* (New York: Peter Lang Publisher, 2004). There is an inscription of Vico

the August Protector of the Roman Catholic Religion, Charles has supported throughout Italy programs of public instruction, thanks to which the witty mind (*ingenium*) of a Neapolitan citizen had the opportunity of meditating on the establishment of a *New Science about the Nature of Nations*. This demonstrates that the system of the natural law of nations derived from that science is suitable to this monarch's kingdom and it is demonstrated to be true in this book which is small for its size but great for the topic hereby considered. For this reason, Giambattista Vico, Professor of Eloquence in the Royal University of Naples, with obsequiousness has presented, given and dedicated to Charles of Austria this glorious legal claim which, within the modest limits of the thought expressed in the book itself, asserts the religiousness of the great fatherland, the

---

for one of the four arches of the funerary chapel for Empress Eleanor, Charles's mother, that is an eulogy of Charles. See *Autobiography*, p. 177: "You citizens, whose great joy is in Charles your noble prince and emperor, let your sorrow be as great in the death of her imperial highness his mother Eleanor, who by her blessed fruitfulness gave you your great desire, a prince of the House of Austria, and by the rare and splendid examples of her queenly virtues gave you your greatest desire, a prince of noble character." In a letter of 1731, with the list and the description of his works and achievements, Vico petitioned this Emperor and King of Naples for an ecclesiastical benefit or pension for his son Gennaro. In another letter of 1729 to the Viceroy of Naples, he referred to Charles VI as "nostro augustissimo regnante imperador Carlo VI d'Austria sia egli principe per zelo di religione e per amor di giustizia gloriosissimo," which are words expressing the same concepts that are found in the dedication.

dignity of the Italic wisdom, the truth of the Roman Catholic church and the majesty of the Emperor King in his full right as monarch, against an anonymous vagabond called herein to judgment at the seat of the *Acta Eruditorum* of Leipzig.

> *Quibus unus metus, si intelligere viderentur*
> (For them there would be fear if they could know him well)
> (Tacitus, *Annals*, bk. 1, v. 11)[9]

---

[9] Vico has chosen this saying from Tacitus in order to alert the erudites of Leipzig (*quibus*) of the danger *(unus metus)* of being deceived whenever they are not fully convinced of the honesty of their correspondents (*si intelligere viderentur*). The dictum points to the heart of the issue presented in this writing.

ABOUT THE BOOK AND ITS REVIEW

[pars. 1–19, a-p]

[1] O most excellent literati of Leipzig, a true friend on this August 1729 has brought me the news that among the book reviews in your issue of the *Acta* of August 1727 there is one that gives wrong information about my book and me. He brought a copy of the *Acta* of August of that year and pointed out where I could read the following.

[2] "In the ... city of Naples a volume *in octavo* has been published (a) with the title of *Principles of a New Science*, (b) whose author, though (c) its name was not revealed to the erudites, (d, e) we came to know from an Italian friend that (f) he is a certain Neapolitan abbé (g) by the name of Vico. In this book the author tried to build (h) a new system of natural law, or (i, j) rather a figment of such a system, greatly different from the one that (k) philosophers have presented heretofore. This new system (l) is deduced from principles (m) truly in conformity with the nature and spirit (*ingenium*) proper of the Church of Rome. The author has (n) with great energy challenged (o) the principles of the doctrines of Grotius and Pufendorf (p);

55   DE LIBRO RELATIO ET IUDICIUM

[1] Quidam verus amicus noster, hoc circumagente mense
Augusto a. mdccxxix, mihi renunciavit inter vestra « Nova literaria » mensis Augusti anni mdccxxvii me meumque librum
a vobis, clarissimi literati Lipsienses viri, sinistre exceptum
60   esse eiusque anni volumen ad me detulit in quo haec quae sequuntur mihi legenda exhibuit.
[2] [2r 10] Prodiit ibidem (Neapoli) liber cui tit. « Principii d'una Scienza nuova » (a) 8° (b), cuius libri auctor, quamvis nomen suum eruditos celet (c), certiores tamen facti sumus
65   per amicum (d) quendam Italum (e) esse eundem abbatem (f)
Neapolitanum cui nomen Vici (g) sit. Agitavit auctor in isto
libello novum iuris naturalis systema (h), seu figmentum (i) potius, ex aliis longe quam hactenus sueverunt philosophi (k) principiis deductum magisque ad ingenium (l) pontificiae Ecclesiae
70   (m) accommodatum. Multo labore (n) contra Grotii et Pufendor-

but he yielded (q) to wit (*ingenium*) more than to truth (r). Though he uses a great quantity of conjectures, (s) his argumentation is ineffective, and by the Italians themselves (t) he is taken with apathy rather than a favorable consideration."

A. Purpose of [these] notes

[3] All these things are indeed false. One thing, however, I would say may be true and it is the fact that your criticism can be viewed as an act of consideration in my regard and this honors me greatly. I intend, therefore, to show with my notes that the source of information on which you relied in publicizing my work and myself was misleading.

B. The notes

[4] In giving the title of my book (a) you have neglected to say that the proper topic of that science is the nature of nations, which any good reviewer of a new publication should have clearly stated with proper emphasis from the beginning of the announcement.

[5] Your friendly correspondent has given you (b) the wrong size of the book, which is *in duodecimo* and not *in octavo*.

[6] Even more necessary was to clarify that since the beginning of the first pages (c) the name Giambattista Vico is repeated twice and again is repeated in the dedication to

fii (o) doctrinas et principia disputat (p); ingenio (q) tamen magis indulget quam veritati (r); longaque coniecturarum mole sibi ipsi deficiens (s), ab ipsis Italis taedio (t) magis quam applausu excipitur.

75   NOTARUM PROPOSITIO

[3] Quae cum sint falsa omnia, praeter unum verum, de quo ibi me reprehendi in eo mecum praeclarissime actum putaverim, his « Notis » ostendam vos aliena fraude deceptos evulgasse.

80   NOTAE

[4] [2v] (a) Sed ipsius Scientiae proprium subiectum, quod est de nationum natura, vasto silentio praeteritur, quod sane novam rem literariam narranti diserte erat et quidem in primis plane enunciandum.

85   [5] (b) Iste qui haec nunciat eius libelli ne formam quidem aspexit, quae est non $8°$ sed $12°$.

[6] (c) Sed in primis eius libri paginis bis meum « Ioh. Baptistae Vici » nomen palam perscripsi: semel in epistola dedicatoria ad eminentissimum cardinalem Corsinium, iterum ubi

90 ad omnes Europae Academias eum librum dirigo.

[7] (d) Ah vere, Germani viri, etiam atque etiam videte ne iste vester simulatus amicus sit, qui talibus rerum literariarum falsissimis nunciis vestram bonam fidem ludibrio habet

Cardinal Corsini, when I recommend the book to the consideration of all the Academies of Europe.

[7] Ah, truly, O German Academicians, be careful and do not be deceived by this supposed friend of yours, (d) who with false information on literary matters would deceive your good faith and make you object of ridicule and legally responsible for publishing in the *Acta* things that are manifestly false.

[8] Really (e) I cannot convince myself that your friend and correspondent is an Italian gentleman. I am rather inclined to think of him as someone from across the Alps, who for his jealousy of the glory and fame of Italy and hate for the Roman Catholic religion, has concocted these lies about my book and me. By the way, where can you find an Italian who would say that this system of natural law so consonant with the Roman Catholic religion has been received with apathy by the Italians who are all Roman Catholic? Therefore, given that this gentleman pretends to be of a different nationality than his own, I should refer to him in these notes as "the vagabond."[10]

[9] For your information, (f) I have been married for

---

[10] Who is this true friend of Vico (*quidam verus amicus noster*)? No scholar has identified him, but at the same time nobody has identified the Italian friend of the literati of Leipzig (*amicus quidam Italus*), the one to whom Vico will often refer as unknown vagabond (*ignotus erro*). The term "vagabond" should here mean "someone without attachment to country or fatherland."

95   eamque sic illudit ut, per tam manifesta mendacia, vos enor-
     miter falsa pro veris temere accepisse ab « Actis » vestris ipsis
     liquido reos peragat.

        [*8*] (e) Sed ego animum inducere nullo pacto possum ut
     istum hominem esse Italum credam; quin potius transalpinum
     aliquem putaverim, prae Italicae gloriae invidia et religionis
100 Romano-catholicae odio, isthaec vobis de me meoque libro
     retulisse. Nam qui Italus sit qui systema de iure naturali gentium
     Romano-catholicae religioni conveniens dicat ab Italis, qui om-
     nes sunt Romano-catholici, cum taedio exceptum esse? Qua-
     propter, cum iste obscurus innominatusque homo gentem fingat
105 alienam, abneget suam, eum in his « Notis » ego « ignotum er-
     ronem » appellabo.

        [*9*] (f) Ego vero uxorem triginta abhinc annis duxi, qua-
     cum concordi adhuc animo vivo et ex qua quinque filios habeo
     superstites. Sed iste ignotus erro de industria heic et fallit et
110 fallitur, ne fortasse in suspicionem veniat quod is me satis et
     noscat et sciat. An potius iste me neque scit neque noscit, quia
     Neapolitanus esse non potest qui ideo me abbatem confingit
     quia systema de iure naturali Romano-catholicae religioni con-
     sonum excogitavi? Quasi vero literati viri Neapolitani doctri-
115 nam suae religioni ii soli submittant qui sunt ex ordine cleri-
     corum! Sitne hinc civis qui in suam patriam tanta impietate
     peccaverit?

        [*10*] (g) Sed ignobilitatem sive obscuritatem mei nominis,
     ut alia documenta praeteream, cognoscite, quaeso, in « Biblio-
120 theca antiqua et nova » domini Ioh. Clerici, ubi, in volu-

thirty years with a woman with whom I still live and with whom I had children of which five are still living.[11] This anonymous vagabond seems to be lying on purpose so that we would not know that he is perhaps someone who knows me well. But is this possible? He cannot be a Neapolitan since he described me as an abbé who has constructed a system of natural law wholly consonant with the Roman Catholic religion. Does he believe that the members alone of the clergy embrace a doctrine in agreement with their religion? Is there a citizen so impious who would renege his own country?

[10] About (g) the irrelevance and obscurity of my name, though leaving unmentioned many other documents, let us point out that Jean Le Clerc discussed extensively some of my writings in the second part of volume 18, article 8, of *Bibliothéque Ancienne et Moderne*.[12] In addition, you can learn from the life of

---

[11] In his addition to the *Autobiography* of Vico, the Marquis of Villarosa describes "those vexations and distresses that a fortunate father is not infrequently compelled to undergo." See *ibid.*, pp. 200–204, where a judgment is made on the wife of Vico, Teresa Caterina Destito, and on three of his children, Luisa, Ignazio, and Gennaro.

[12] Le Clerc's review concluded, "… we gather that the author is regarded as an expert in metaphysics, law and philology, and his work as original and full of important discoveries." Other sentences of Le Clerc are gathered together by Vico in the *Autobiography* (pp. 164–165). The correspondence between Le Clerc and Vico is spare: one of Le Clerc the 8 September, 1722, in which Jean thanks Vico for the copy of *De Uno* and *De Constantia* (available in the *Autobiography*, p. 159 and in

minis XVIII parte altera, articulo VIII, de quibusdam meis
libris plurimum sermonem habet; cognoscite ex mea ipsius « Vita », quam, a me per me ipsum scriptam, enixe flagitavit clarus
vir comes Iohannes Articus de Porcia, eminentiss. cardinalis de
125 Porcia germanus frater, quae Venetiis, me invito, [3r] ut ipse
eius vulgator ibi palam profitetur, extat in « Opusculorum
Eruditorum collectione » reverendi patris Calogerá, in cuius calce « Catalogus » attexitur librorum quos triginta perpetuos annos, ab quo iam inde usque tempore in regia Neapolitana Aca-
130 demia eloquentiam profiteor, et ultra etiam id tempus, lucubravi.

[*11*] (h) Atqui non ius naturale gentium est primarium
eius Scientiae subiectum sed communis nationum natura, ex qua
constans et universa rerum divinarum atque humanarum notitia apud omnes aeque populos defluit diffluitque; unde no-
135 vum de iure naturali systema invenitur, quod est eius Scientiae
quoddam praecipuum corollarium.

[*12*] (i) Videte cui figmenta displiceant, severo scilicet phi-
losopho, qui de me meoque et nomine et statu et ordine et
libro tot et tanta confingit! Sed omittamus hominem et rem
140 ipsam pensemus. Igitur doctrinas et principia pontificiae Ecclesiae accommodata iste ignotus erro, hoc suo dicto « figmenta »,
coniecturarum mole sibi male cohaerentia atque adeo ineptas
fabulas putat? Quis, non dico Neapolitanus, non dico Italus,
sed quivis Romano-catholicus suae verae religioni tam male-
145 dixerit?

[*13*] (k) Quorsumnam ignotus erro isthaec dicit? An quia
Grotius et Pufendorfius, addatur cumulo etiam quoque Seldenus, tres eius doctrinae principes, isti erroni videntur ii soli
esse philosophi, quia nemo omnium est Romano-catholicus? An
150 vero ut significet me non esse philosophum? Quod si is id

---

Universal Right, p. 724); two of Vico, dated 9 January 1722 and
18 October 1723 (available in *Universal Right*, pp. 723 and 725).

59

myself written by myself on the insistent request of the most distinguished Gian Artico Porcia, brother of His Eminence the Cardinal de Porcia. This autobiography, against my own desire, was made part of the *Opusculorum Eruditorum Collectio* of the Rev. Father Calogerá, who added first to it a catalogue of the books that I have written and explained that for thirty years I have been teaching eloquence to the students of the Royal University of Naples.[13]

[11] The primary topic (h) of the science [discussed in the book] is not the natural law of nations but the common nature of nations, from which a constant and universal knowledge of things divine and human originates and is diffused. Consequently, a new system of natural law is found that is the true principal corollary of that science.

[12] Now you tell me (i, j) who is the serious philosopher who has fabricated so many things about me, my name, my status, and my book! But let us forget the man and think instead of the thoughts he expressed. Does this anonymous vagabond really believe that the doctrines and the principles in accordance with the Church of Rome are, as he said, figments of imagination, a pile of badly

---

[13] Vico's *Autobiography* was a successful book and became a model in the literary field of autobiographical writings. He himself was manifestly very pleased with it. A kind of commentary to the Vichian autobiography was composed by Philip D. Verene, *Giambattista Vico and the New Art of Autobiography*.

sentiat, eorum duum alterum is hoc suo dicto significat: aut
quod is me, si cum doctis nescit, saltem cum vulgo noscit non
esse philosophiae sed philologiae, nempe eloquentiae, professo-
rem, quia cum vulgo putat eloquentiam a philosophia esse rem
155   prorsus aliam; aut quod is eum librum omnino non legerit,
cuius perpetua haec ratio est, ut philologiam — sive rerum omnium quae ab libero hominum arbitrio dependent, ut sunt lin-
guarum, morum et rerum sive pace actarum sive bello gestarum
historiae, universam doctrinam — philosophiae, ut par est et ne-
160   mo hactenus tentavit philosophus, submittam et, ab exploratis
philosophiae principiis, philologiam in certam scientiae formam
redigam. An quia in eo systemate ius monarchicum rationibus
firmo quas hactenus non videre philosophi? Si id sentiat erro
iste, is implacabiliter pugnantia planissime dicit. Sic enim Gro-
165   tium, qui isti in hoc ipso argumento est philosophus, pro quo
stare profitetur, non solum deserit sed oppugnat. Nam non
alio sane consilio Gronovius in Grotium suas « Notas » scripsit
quam ut scriberet accommodate ad ingenium popularis
Batavorum libertatis, qui eum auctorem, ut assentatorem
170   monarchiae, notat. An merito? Non est hic disserendi locus.
Uter igitur scribit ad alterius ingenium accommodate, quod
Tacito illud elegans est ' per ambitionem ', quod esset Italice
vertendum « a compiacenza », egone, qui ex vero quod Ecclesia
catholica docet quodque Grotius etiam agnoscit, an erro iste,
175   ut vestrae populari Lipsiensium libertati morem gerat?

[*14*] Ceterum, cur iste me e sueta philosophorum via excessisse dicat non plane intelligo, nisi forsan quia id systema in
Divinae [3v] Providentiae principio fundandum curavi; quod
Grotius omnino non fecit, qui, omni Dei opt. max. cognitione
180   praecisa, suum systema constare palam profitetur; Pufendorfius
quidem fecit, sed, data hypothesi prorsus Epicurea hominis sine
ulla divina ope, consilio, in hunc mundum coniecti, quo nomine

coherent conjectures, or useless fables? Who is the Neapolitan, or rather the Italian, or the Roman Catholic person who would speak so badly of his own religion?

[13] Why is this unknown vagabond saying these things? Is it perhaps (k) because only Grotius and Pufendorf, and let us add also Selden, the three non-Roman Catholic princes of this doctrine, appeared to him as the only true philosophers?[14] Or is he saying that I am not a philosopher? If he really intends this then two are the possible meanings of his statement. First, he may know that I am a professor of philology, that is eloquence, and not of philosophy. Now then, not being like the learned but rather like the common people he may believe that eloquence is something else than philosophy. Second, he may have not read my book at all. The continuous theme of the book is my attempt at showing how philology—the general doctrine of all that pertains to human free choice, like languages, customs, and the history of deeds done in time of peace or war—is philosophy, as it should rightly be. No philosopher heretofore has attempted this, but from serious studying of philosophy's principles, I could assign to

---

[14] [Huig van Groot (Grotius, 1583–1645), the famous author of *De Iure Belli ac Pacis libri tres* (1625). John Selden (Seldenius, 1584–1654) is the author of *De Iure Naturali et Gentium iuxta Disciplinam Hebraeorum*. Samuel Pudendorf (Pufendorfius, 1632–1694) is the author of *De Iure Naturali et Gentium*.] Grotius is also known in Vichian scholarship as "the fourth author" (see the reason for this in *Autobiography*, pp. 154–155).

a doctis aeque ac piis accusatus, dissertatione ad id edita caussam dicere adactus est. Ego vero praeterea Divinae Providen-
185 tiae placito et illud quoque adstruo consentaneum homini li-
beram esse recti pravique electionem, sine quibus philosophiae
principiis de iustitia, de iusto, de legibus disseri omnino quicquam non potest. Si erro iccirco me e sueta philosophorum via
excessisse ait, is certe Platonem, qui Divinam Providentiam in
190 suis placitis statuit et liberum homini turpis honestique arbi-
trium vindicat, per summam licentiam, quae furori proxima esset, divinum philosophum ex albo philosophorum eraderet.
Quod si forte ita sit, is se ultro novatorem accusat; nam nemo
sane alius reprehenderet nostrum systema, quod sit ad inge-
195 nium pontificiae Ecclesiae accommodatum, nisi qui, Lutheri
aut Calvini assecla, Stoicorum sectam et fatum in Christianam
philosophiam intrudit et in servo hominis arbitrio caecam necessitatem seu premere sive opprimere cuncta decreverit.

[15] (l) Non temere heic ab errone vox « ingenium » de-
200 lecta; ea enim exprimit linguae genium, qua novatores loquun-
tur, quum dicunt quod Ecclesia Romano-catholica disputatio-
num ingenio, non instrumenti, hoc est Evangelii, veritate nita-
tur; et idem deinceps iccirco me, in eo systemate magis ad ingenium pontificiae Ecclesiae accommodato, ait magis ingenio
205 indulgere quam veritati.

[16] (m) Praeclarum vero id mihi imputo, tantum abest
ut quicquam inde graver. Quidni systema meum illi Ecclesiae
accommodarem quae veritatem suis indigitat professoribus?

philology the undeniable form of science. Or is it because in the system introduced in that book I justify the legitimacy of monarchy, the *jus monarchicum*, with some unprecedented reasons, which were unheard of for the aforementioned philosophers? If this is what this vagrant is affirming, then he certainly contradicts himself. In fact, in this same argument he considers Grotius to be a philosopher with whom he agrees, but by so doing he moves away from Grotius and even opposes him. You must know that Gronovius when writing to the people of Holland wrote according to their love of liberty and for that purpose made his comments on Grotius as a supporter of monarchy. Was this accurate? This is not the place to discuss it. Anyway, who of the two writes in order "to please, to gain favors"—a behavior Tacitus referred to with the expression "*per ambitionem*" which was rendered in Italian as "*a compiacenza*"—I, who according to truth wrote what the Catholic Church teaches and that Grotius himself recognizes, or this vagabond who writes to please the people of Leipzig who are very proud of their custom of popular liberty? [15]

[14] I do not understand why this vagabond is saying

---

[15] [Johann Friedrich Gronow (Gronovius, 1611–1671), a philologist, the most famous commentator on *De Iure Belli ac Pacis* of Grotius.] Vico said of the comments of Gronovius that they were written "more to please free governments than to give justice its due."

Immo vero ipsa se mihi commodam praebuit ad id constabilien-
210 dum systema universo generi humano accommodatum, quae me
illa dogmata docuit duo, alterum de Divina Providentia, alterum
de libero hominis arbitrio, in quae duo universum genus humanum consentit, ita ut adversus ea ipsi sive Lutheri sive Calvini sectatores verba palam facere prohibeantur; uti Theodoro
215 Bezae semel accidit in Helvetiis, ubi principem Calvini locum
tenuit, qui, cum eius modi concionem habuisset, ita omnis Chri-
stiani officii recte faciendi auditores animum despondere, ut
adversus ea catholica dogmata in posterum praedicare a magi-
stratu vetitus sit.
220   [*17*] (n) An iste ignotus erro est ariolus, qui id de me
fatetur verum? [4r] Nam in eo systemate tentando, firmando
adornandoque, qui per erronem istum ipsum ingenio nimis in-
dulgeo, triginta ferme vitae annos insumpserim.
    [*18*] (o) Hoc verbum erro vobis iniecit ut, vestratis Pu-
225 fendorfii caussa, is apud vos invidiam libro conflaret; quo non
minus vos ad indignationem commovendos esse arbitrabatur
quam illo, systema potius ad ingenium pontificiae Ecclesiae
accommodatum. Sed vos, iustos aequosque rerum literariarum
aestimatores, haud sane decet in librorum censura prae partium
230 studiis ne latum quidem unguem transversos agi.
    [*19*] (p) Nam cur Seldenum omisit, tertium sed tempore
secundum eius tractationis principem, contra cuius quoque

that I went astray from the usual way of thinking of philosophers, unless it is because I cared to found my system on divine providence. Grotius certainly did not, because he testified that his system is very well-founded even without the knowledge of the existence of God Almighty. Pufendorf on the contrary did it, but only in an added dissertation after having been accused by learned and religious people of Epicureanism for having cast man into the world bereft of divine care and assistance. On the other hand, beside the intervention of the divine providence, I admit what is proper to man, by which I mean the free election of good and evil. Without these two philosophic principles no man would be able to speak of justice, right, and laws. If, therefore, this tramp said that I have abandoned the usual way of philosophizing, in his extreme madness, he should also certainly erase from the album of philosophers the name of Plato, the divine philosopher, who among his assumptions has placed divine providence and has attributed to man free choice of the honest or dishonest. If this is how things really are, then this individual is revealing himself as one of the innovators. Could there be anyone else who would criticize my system for being consonant with the beliefs of the Church of Rome other than someone who, as a follower of Luther or Calvin, would place among the principles of a Christian philosophy those of the Stoics and fate, and dogmatically recognize in

doctrinas et principia disputo, quod suum de iure naturali systema Noachicum ex Providentiae principio, rationibus ab ipso
235   divinarum humanarumque rerum ordine naturaliter deductis,
non constabiliat? Vah! nunc iam intelligo. Huic erroni non
videtur Seldenus philosophus, quia is ex sacro « Geneseos »
libro Providentiam supponit. Igitur neque isti erroni est philosophus Cicero, qui negat se posse cum Attico disserere quic-
240   quam de legibus nisi ille id sibi det, quod universum hominum
genus communi sensu sibi habet persuasum, humana cuncta
nobis a Divina Providentia recte riteque dispensari. Unde
Grotius videat an suum systema, omni Dei opt. max. cognitione praecisa, verum sit! Et videant eruditi Romani iuris
245   interpretes an recte sectas Stoicam et Epicuream in Romanam
iurisprudentiam invitas compellant, quae, in suis « Institutio-
nibus » ius naturale gentium definit ius a Divina Providentia
constitutum! [4v] Adeone iste ignotus erro Divinae Providentiae impium bellum indicit, cui aeque non sint philosophi
250   et Cicero, qui eam esse numen rerum humanarum conscium
ex communi omnium gentium et populorum consensu vult
credi, et Plato, qui eam esse ordinem rerum naturalium in-
telligentem ac liberum naturalibus rationibus dissertavit!

DE HUMANO INGENIO, ACUTE ARGUTEQUE DICTIS ET DE RISU
255   E RE NATA DIGRESSIO.

[20] (q) Sed philosophia, geometria, philologia atque
adeo omnia doctrinarum genera istam opinionem, ingenium cum
veritate pugnare, absurdissimam esse manifesto convincunt.

the lack of free will the existence of a blind necessity that presses and oppresses all things?[16]

[15] Not by chance (l) our vagabond has used the word *ingenium* (ingenuity, wit, perspicacity). The root of this word expresses the language's perspicacious ability to adapt or *linguae genium* which the innovators refer to in their speech when they affirm that the Roman-Catholic Church in its argumentation uses an ingenious or ambiguous rather than a language based on truth, that is, on the Gospel. For this reason, he stated that in my system I used an ingenious language in conformity with the positions of the Roman Church rather than in conformity with truth.

[16] But I am proud of what I wrote (m) and I find no fault. Why shouldn't I build a system in agreement with the Church that teaches the truth to its membership? Truly it was this church that gave me the suggestion to formulate a system suitable to all humankind; it was this church that taught me those two doctrines, the one of the divine providence and the other of human free will. All humankind agrees on these two principles and even the followers of Luther and Calvin were forbidden to speak against them.

---

[16] The text: *Quod si forte ita sit, is se ultro novatorem accusat.* He manifests himself to be a reformer, says Vico, and the names of the two major agents of the Reformation are given, Martin Luther and Jean Calvin, with a summary sentence on their doctrines.

[21] Et principio philosophia; namque non solum vulgo
260 dicitur sed philosophis quoque probatur ingenium esse divinum omnium inventionum parentem. Atque utinam philosophiae opera daretur cum Verulamii « Organo », ut, quod
philosophi meditarentur, id ii verum esse experimentis ipsis
demonstrarent, uti cum « Organo » suo idem Verulamius li-
265 brum cui titulus « Cogitata ⟨et⟩ visa » lucubravit! Cogitandi sane ars sive scientia Anglorum cognata vel ab antiquis usque tem-
poribus, quibus sapiens Agricola, apud Tacitum in eius « Vita », ut eos ad humanitatis excolendas artes impelleret 'Bri-
tannorum ingenia studiis Gallorum' a n t e f e r e b a t ; unde
270 apud Anglos etiam nunc praeter ceteras philosophia experimen-
talis celebratur. Nam, si ita physicae incumberetur, non solum
non pluris fierent a Socrate sutores quam sophistae, cum illi
tamen aliquod faciant opus humano generi utile, hi vero nullum omnino, sed in eo sane Deo opt. max. quodammodo
275 similes fierent, cuius intelligentia et opus unum idemque sunt.
[22] [5r] Geometriam autem, etsi ego a limine salu-
tavi,introspexi tamen synthetica antiquorum methodo innu-
meras Euclidis propositiones, quae sunt magnitudinum elementa, percurrere easque legere quae, distractae ac dissipatae,
280 nullum inter se πρός τι, vernacula lingua « rapporto », habere
prius videbantur; atque ex iis elementis non in problematis
solum, quae circino et regula, saltem mente factis, construit,
sed vel in theorematis ipsis, quae vera contemplatur eam facere
vera. Quod sane praestare nequit nisi qui praestanti ingenio
285 praeditus sit; unde geometra in illo suo figurarum mundo
est quidam deus, uti Deus opt. max. in hoc mundo animo-
rum et corporum est quidam geometra. Et sane qui geome-

This was the case of Theodorus Beza in Switzerland, where he succeeded to Calvin in the leadership of the Reformation. In one of his sermons speaking on a topic dealing with these two principles he expressed himself in such a way that the audience despaired to be ever able to rightly perform all Christian duties. For this reason, the magistrate legislated the preaching against these catholic doctrines to be hereafter forbidden.

[17] Is it possible (n) that this vagabond is an augur who tells the truth about me? He is saying that in the building, ordering, reviewing of my system I indulged greatly on ingenuity (*ingenium*) for thirty years of my life.[17]

[18] This vagabond (o) has convinced you to reject my book because it criticized one of your countryman, Pufendorf, and he makes you hate me more for this than for having written things agreable to the Church of Rome. You, however, who judge literary production with justice and equanimity, you know very well how to be totally impartial in your assessment of books.

[19] But, why has he omitted Selden, (p) the third prince of this doctrine, although he was second in time for the publication of his treatise on the subject? It is also

---

[17] The text: *An iste ignotus erro est ariolus, qui id de me fatetur verum? Ariolus* is a soothsayer who makes use of *ariolation* in soothsaying. Why is Vico using the term *ariolus*? After all he confirms that indeed he spent thirty years of his life in meditating on this new science of 1725.

290 triam in mechanicae usus delapsam ad opera sive urbana sive militaria efficienda profitentur, apud nos Italos, momentoso et scientiae referto vocabulo, vocantur « *ingegnieri* ». Nec quae de synthetica dicimus, analytica methodus quicquam obturbat, quae ex quadam divina ingenii occulta vi nata est, qua ipsi algebristae divinari sibi videntur quum suis rationibus recte subductis vera demonstrant; et quae saepe synthetici labo-
295 riorissime praestarent, eā ipsā analytici expediti ac faciles atque adeo solertes efficiunt; quae, nisi quaedam ingenii vis humana maior sit, alia sane esse non potest.

[*23*] In physica vero, cuius medicina est appendix, iam docuimus, in politica, ad quam senatoria, imperatoria, ora-
300 toria et iurisprudentia revocantur, mox, in specie de oratoria, planum faciemus eos unos solertia praecellere qui ingenio plu- rimum possunt. In una theologia, quam ab Dei opt. max., qui Primum Verum est, divino ingenio docemur, nos nostrum hominum infirmum ingenium [*5v*] disperdere, illiusque vera,
305 humanum captum exsuperantia, magis quam quae sunt geo- metricis apodixibus demonstrata credere vera fas est, cum ex quadam minima illius divina ingenii particula, humanum cap- tum quoque etiam, ut diximus, excedente, algebra sua indubia vera demonstret.

310 [*24*] Postremo philologia in rhetoricis docet ingenii acu- men sine veritate stare non posse, quod res quae, distractae dissitaeque, quam longissime vulgo videbantur in aliquam la- tentis veri communem rationem stringit et acuit, in qua, com- plurium longarum ratiocinationum compendio facto, res illae
315 concinno inter se nexu aptae colligataeque esse deteguntur. Unde Aristoteles rationem affert cur tantopere acuta dicta de-

against Selden's doctrine and principles I discussed, because he does not solidly establish his Noachian system of natural law on the principle of providence with reasons naturally deduced from the order of human and divine things.[18] Yes, I understand now. Selden for our vagabond is not a philosopher because he assumed providence relying on the sacred book of *Genesis*. But then, not even Cicero is a philosopher for this vagabond! Cicero denied that he could discuss with Atticus about laws unless Atticus could be persuaded of what is commonly felt by all humankind that all human things are rightly and properly dispensed by divine providence. Hence, Grotius should reflect whether his system would still be true, if he would rule out the cognition of God Almighty.

The learned interpreters of Roman laws should also reflect if it is right to urge the unwilling sects, Epicurean and Stoic, to [accept] the Roman jurisprudence, which in its Institutes defines the natural law of nations a law constituted by divine providence!

---

[18] [The Noachian system is the system of the natural or universal law of peoples, and the adjective *noachicus* was coined by Vico from the term *Noachida* (son of Noah) used by Selden in his *De Iure Naturali et Gentium iuxta Disciplinam Hebraeorum* (Argentorati 1665, p. 115). Selden writes: "I have many times mentioned that all the precepts regarding all of humankind are called *The precepts of the Noachians*, that is, of the sons or descendants of Noah. With this term *Noachian* can be signified the Hebrews, but with regard to origin also all the other nations. Nonetheless the Hebrew peoples would consider themselves superior to all other peoples because privileged by God."]

How far is this anonymous vagabond carrying his impious war against divine providence? For him, neither Cicero would be a philosopher because he believed with the common consent of all peoples and nations that divine providence is a deity conscious of all human events, nor Plato who argued with reasons based on natural things that divine providence is an intelligent and free order of natural things!

lectent: quia mens, suapte natura veri famelica, acuto dicto audito, in brevi summa, temporis momento, complura discit.

[25] Contra, arguta dicta finguntur ab infirma brevique
320 phantasia, quae aut nuda nomina rerum confert aut solas rerum superficies, neque totas, componit aut aliqua sive absurda sive inepta menti nec-opinanti obiicit, quae, expectans conveniens et aptum, sua expectatione deluditur et frustratur; unde cerebri fibrillae, ad aptum et conveniens obiectum in-
325 tentae et ab alio non expectato turbatae, tumultuantur, atque ita turbantes trepidum motum suum per ipsorum truncum in omnes nervorum ramos dispergunt; qui motus totum corpus concutit hominemque de suo recto statu deturbat. Ex quo fit ut bruta animantia expertia risus sint, quia singularem
330 sensum habent quo ad singula obiecta singillatim attendunt, quorum quodque ab alio sese belluae obiiciente discutitur et deletur: [6r] ex qua una re perspicue palam facias, ipso risus sensu belluis a natura negato, eas omnis esse expertes rationis. Atque heic certe, nec sane alibi, occultus ille risoribus
335 sensus subest, qui eos ipsos latet, quum seria risu excipiunt: quod, cum risus sit proprius hominis, quum id faciunt, tunc vero ii se sibi hominem sapere videantur. Sed risus est ex illa nostra hominum natura infirma qua

‘ decipimur specie recti ’.

340 Namque, ex hac risus a nobis sic explicata natura, inter severos gravesque viros et belluas ridiculi homines sunt quasi medii.

[26] Ridiculorum autem appellatione heic accipio et qui temere ac immodeste rident, qui proprie « risores » appellandi

THIS DIGRESSION DERIVES FROM THE ABOVE NOTES AND DEALS WITH HUMAN INGENUITY, ACUTE AND ARGUTE SAYINGS, AND LAUGHTER
[pars. 20–31, q]

[20] I begin by saying that (q) philosophy, geometry, philology, and all other branches of knowledge clearly prove that this opinion on the conflict of ingenuity (*ingenium*) with truth (*veritas*) is absolutely absurd.

[21] Considering philosophy, we may say that the common folks, as well as the philosophers, all of them accept ingenuity as the divine genitor of inventions. Would the heavens that peoples would engage in philosophy in the way suggested by Bacon in the *Novum Organum* so that what the philosophers conceived they also demonstrate its truth with experiments.[19] Bacon himself acted coherently with the suggestions in the *Organum* when he composed the book titled *Cogitata et Visa*! Truly, the art or science of thinking is quite familiar to the English since ancient times, when the wise Agricola, as Tacitus narrates in the *Life of Agricola*, so to induce them to care

---

[19] Francis Bacon (1561–1626) published the *Novum Organum* in 1620. Vico admired Bacon greatly, saying that "he was a man of incomparable wisdom" and elected him as the third of his four authors (*Autobiography*, p. 139). In all his writings, Vico would mention the doctrines of Bacon with words of praise and admiration for his contributions.

345 sunt, et qui ad risum alios commovent, qui proprie appellan-
tur « derisores ». Etenim severi non rident, quia ad unum graviter attendunt nec ab alio inde deturbantur; belluae neque
etiam rident, quia attendunt ad unum quoque, sed, ab alio
tactae, ad illud totae protinus convertuntur; risores vero, quia
350 leviter attendunt ad unum, inde facile deturbantur ab alio.
Derisores autem longissime a viris gravibus abscedunt et
quam proxime accedunt ad belluas, qui ipsam veri speciem
depravant, nec solum depravant sed pervertunt; et, vi quadam sibi suaeque menti et vero facta, de qua loquitur para-
355 situs Gnato ubi, apud comicum, inquit:

> ...' postremo imperavi egomet mihi
> Omnia assentari ',

quod unum in se est contorquent ad aliud. Quod verum poëtae
suis fabulis abdidere, qui, cum tales homines inter viros et
360 belluas sint quasi medii, satyros risores confixerunt.
　　[27] Hinc derisoribus, ex sua ipsorum hac perversa natura
semper veri egenis, divini veritatis thesauri semper occlusi sunt;
et quum vera et severa deridendo sibi plaudunt, tunc illud
Divinae Sapientiae verbum vere in eos accidit: ' Si sapiens
365 fueris, tibi ' i p s e　f u e r i s ; ' si ' derisor, tu ' solus ' damnum
' portabis '. Ex hac item risus explicata natura fit quod ridiculae
comoediarum personae validius oblectant quum serio ineptiunt,
uti saepe frigent quae ridendo student ad risum commovere
spectatores. Et sane facetia nusquam lepidior est quam ubi
370 mimi viros severos et graves vultu, incessu et actione imitan-
tur, eaque ratione eos in proscenio deridendos traducunt. Quae
omnia huc redeunt denique, quod risus ex dolo venit qui humano ingenio, veri avido, tenditur, eoque effusior venit unde
veri maior est simulatio.
375　　[28] Hinc eleganter et vere Cicero dixit risus sedem esse
subturpe, non improbiter turpe, ut enormiter falsum, quale est

and cultivate the humanities, said to prefer their ingenuity (*ingenium*) to the erudition (*eruditio*) of the French. Consequently, the English still now favor experimental philosophy. For Socrates the cobblers were more valuable than the sophists, because cobblers make things useful to humankind while sophists make nothing at all, but in this [doing experimental philosophy] they could somehow become similar to God Almighty whose understanding is one and identical with making.[20]

[22] As for geometry, though I only stopped at its door, I confess to have examined with the synthetic method of the ancients innumerable propositions of Euclid, which are like the elements of the geometric figures. Geometry shows what in vulgar language we call rapport between dimensions that previously, as they were separate and distinct, appeared to have nothing in common. From the elements, geometry with a pair of compasses and a ruler finds the solution of problems constructed by the mind, and in the theoretical problems in which the mind gazes upon the truth, geometry makes it true. This is something that only he who is gifted with an excellent ingenuity can do.

---

[20] The Roman historian Tacitus is the second chosen or preferred author of Vico. Vico made his own all the theories of his four authors and their inspirations formed and guided him in the writing of his works and the creation of his theories. In the following notes Vico condenses many descriptions of the modern sciences and refers to the one principle *verum ipsum factum*, which is the basic principle of his metaphysics of 1710 and his inaugural oration of 1708.

quiddam contrarium et, multo magis, aliquod sui negans, quod scholae dicunt « contradictorium », quod gravi dolore mentem afficit, quae proinde ad improba mendacia irascitur et indigna-
380 tur; sed paullo turpe, ut, quemadmodum acute dictum de eo est quod in speciem videbatur aliud mox idem re ipsa compe-ritur, nemque aliquod verum quod sub falsi latebat imagine, ita dictum argute de eo sit quod videbatur idem, deinde re ipsa aliud esse detegitur, nimirum aliquod falsum quod quan-
385 dam veri speciem prae se ferebat; ex qua specie nec-opinanter obiecta, uti ex quibusdam ridiculis comoediarum personis re-pente visis, risus oboritur, quem Divina Sapientia docet esse in ore stultorum, quia cerebrorum fibrillae in amentibus, qui Latinis satis sapienter mente non constare dicuntur, semper
390 titubant, vacillant, lapsant; quod per conspicuos corporum motus natura ipsa sensu quodam verum esse nos docet, quum, aliorum lapsu casuve conspecto, vulgo homines vix contineri possunt quin rideant.

[29] Hinc, quia haec mentis [6v] imbecillitas stultitiae
395 fundus est, philosophia in eo tota occupatur atque ad id prae-cipuum collimat, ut firmet constantiam sapientis. Indidem in-telligere datur quam diverso voluptatis genere spectatores affi-ciant fabulae recte moratae et quae Latinis erant sive « Oscae » sive « Atellanae », quae nunc nobis « commedie burlesche » vo-
400 cantur. Illae namque voluptatem afferunt sapiente homine di-gnam, cuius mens semper ad uniforme, conveniens et aptum intendit; quae delectatio eadem numero est atque illa qua specta-tor ludi, sit ex genere pilae, perfunditur quum videt, quo lusor iactum intenderat et quo oportuerat, eo pilae aleam cecidisse;
405 quare fabulas recte moratas difficile inveniunt nisi qui in phi-losophiae moralis studio sint plane consummatissimi; fabulae autem ridiculae genere voluptatis oblectant impotenti et effreni, quae homines sanae mentis insanos faciunt, quibus risu omnem rectam resolvunt rationem.

Therefore, the geometrician in his world of figures is a god in the same way that God Almighty in this world of spirits and bodies is a geometrician. For this reason, Italians call with the prestigious scientific term of *ingegnieri* (engineers) those who work with geometry applied to mechanics for the construction of urban or military buildings. What we favorably said about the synthetic method should not minimize the validity of the analytical one that is born from some hidden divine power of ingenuity. The same practicians of algebra sense that they are divining when they arrive to the demonstration of truth with their logically deduced expressions. Often what the users of the synthetic methodology achieve after feverish labour, the users of the analytic process are instead expeditious, facile, and primarily ingenious in accomplishing. Thus, unless there is another greater human power of ingenuity, this is certainly the one.

[23] Of physics, whose appendix is medicine, I implicitly spoke above. As for politics, which comprehends the art of governing, ruling, persuading, and legislating, let me make clear that especially in rhetoric or art of persuading the only one who will excel are those endowed with a great ingenuity. In theology alone, which God Almighty, the First Truth, teaches us with divine ingenuity, we do not use our human limited ingenuity. We should believe the truths of theology although they surpass our

410   [*30*] Quae est ratio cur Demosthenes, orator procul dubio omnium acutissimus, qui ea incomparabili dicendi ratione perpetuo utebatur ut auditores ab proposita caussa in res alias, quam maxime longinquas, averteret et abduceret, ita ut illi quo Demosthenes errabundus evaderet mirarentur, is interea in
415 iis rebus longissime provisis rationem aliquam inveniret quae ad caussam, quam ageret diceretve, esset quodammodo affecta, eamque proposito suo feliciter componeret et aptaret; eaque acutissima dicendi ratione intorquebat curta suo illo dictionis genere rotato enthymemata, quae, fulminum instar, eo vehemen-
420 tiora cadebant quo magis ea fuerant improvisa; unde « orator enthymematicus » dictus est et fulmini a Longino comparatur. Quam [7r] is dicendi rationem, complures annos eius auditor, a Platone didicerat, qui, dialectica Socratica usus, eum quicum de alia re disserebat, de re quae illi videretur alia, interrogabat,
425 et ex eo quod ille sibi, tanquam aliud, dederat, conficiebat id ab illo sibi datum illud ipsum esse de quo cum illo dissertatio erat instituta; quam interrogandi artem (id enim « dialectica » Graecis sonat) philosophorum sapientissimus Socrates excogitavit apposite ad excolendam Graecorum naturam, qui omnes
430 orbis terrarum nationes ingenio superarunt. Is, inquam, Demosthenes, qui acumine tantum valuit, risum nunquam excitare suis orationibus potuit, et, si quando voluit, in eo, ut Cicero tradit, tam ineptus fuit ut ipse potius esset ridiculus.

limited intellect. We should believe them as truths more true than the geometric apodixises which algebra with some minimal divine particle of ingenuity that exceeds the limited human ingenuity uses to demonstrate its indubitable truths.

[24] Then, in the books on rhetoric,[21] philology teaches that acumen of intellect and truth are always joined together, because the acumen brings things—that are separate and scattered and previously appeared to the common folks far different—together and stir them up in some common relationship of a latent truth, in which they are seen aptly connected by a beautiful bond. This is a truth obtained without the multitude of long ratiocinations. Hence Aristotle explains why acute sayings please so greatly: because the mind, by its nature longing for truth, after hearing an acute saying, in an instant, learns many things.

[25] On the contrary, argute sayings are fashioned by a fantasy that is flaccid and short-lived, a fantasy that

---

[21] It is in the *Institutiones Oratoriae* that Vico deals with all aspects of rhetoric and touches on the concepts of acute and argute sayings, but given the earlier composition of those lecture on rhetoric, the digression in the *Vici vindiciae* seems to add some more insights and examples. A comparative analysis of the two texts could be a good subject for future studies. For now, see *The Art of Rhetoric* (Atlanta-Amsterdam: Rodopi, 1996), ch. 37: "On Conceits, or Del Ben Parlare in Concetti." In ch. 27 of the same book, Vico justifies the use of a digression when "it seems to flow spontaneously by itself from the narration."

compares bare names of things, or joins together only some of their superficial characteristics, or presents absurd or inept ones to a dormant mind, which expecting something challenging and apt, is deluded and frustrated in its expectation. And so it happens that the fibers of the brain that were expecting challenge and learning are instead affected by the unexpected deception, become turbulent and transmit their tremble through their main trunk to all the ramification of the nerves. This physical alteration, then, affects the whole body and man experiences a mutation of his normal condition. What we just described about man explains why beasts are deprived of laughter. Beasts possess a specific sense with which they sense each single object singularly, and the sensation of a single object is effaced and deleted as soon as a new one presents itself. I want to make clear another thing related to this, that having nature deprived brutes of laughter, they are rightfully stripped of rationality. It is from this and from nowhere else that a strange feeling pervades those who laugh, a feeling however concealed to those who take serious things with laugh because, since laughter is the proper attribute of man, when they laugh, precisely in the experience of laughing, they truly experience their humanity. The laughter of man, however, is from our infirm nature that "deceives us with the semblance of the just." From this personal explanation of

[*31*] Ex his omnibus iste ignotus erro colligat quantum
435   sit ingenium contrarium veritati, ut nihil aeque atque ingenium
veritatem studiosissime consectetur; quod, quia heic res nata
est, pluribus notavi ut isti erroni adprobarem quam vere is
cum vulgo putet doctrinam de eloquentia a philosophia esse
rem prorsus aliam.

440   [*32*] (r) O veritatis graphycum amatorem, qui formam mei
libri 8°, me in eo meum eruditos celare nomen, meque esse
abbatem palam ac manifesto mentitur! Quod cum magis magisque cogito mecumque animo reputo, demiror sane ut prava
consuetudo rectam hominum naturam non solum depravat sed
445   pervertit. Namque istum ignotum erronem in falsis fictisque
cogitationibus innatum, innutritum, adultum confirmatumque
esse necesse est, qui, uti per ea quae superius de me finxerat,
dixit meum systema esse figmentum, ita heic, per ea quae de
meo libro mentitur, [7v] me non indulgere veritati opinatur.
450   Itaque iste infelix, quam gravi tam misero exemplo, se unum
ex iis hominibus esse probat qui, ut divine divinus Plato di-
cebat, si in antro, ab eius ore aversi, totam vitam traducerent,
cum semper umbras quas in imum antrum proiicerent contem-
plati essent, si forte postea, sic provecta aetate, ad os antri
455   converterentur, extra antrum posita corpora umbras esse perperam perverseque iudicarent.

[*33*] (s) Scilicet in Scientia de communi omnium hominum

laughter I may say that men who act always as jesters (*ridiculi*) do are viewed as standing between serious honorable individuals and brutes.

[26] I call laughers (*ridiculi*) those who laugh inconsiderately and immoderately who should properly be called buffoons (*risores*), and those who make other peoples laugh who should be called mockers or scoffers (*derisores*). Serious persons do not laugh because they attend to one serious activity and do not admit distractions. Brutes do not laugh either because they, too, are drawn by one thing alone, but as soon as another object presents itself they immediately turn their attention to it. As for laughers (the *risores*), since they are lightly involved in one single thing, they can be easily distracted by another. Mockers and scoffers (*derisores*) are the ones most removed from serious persons and come quite near the brutes, because not only they alter the appearance of what is true but they also pervert it. Against their mind and the truth, these individuals use the force about which the parasite Gnatho in Terence's *Eunuchus* (2, 2, 22) says: "I at last forced myself to agree in everything with myself." Thus, they twist the truth of things, at their pleasure. In their fables the poets have hidden the truth about these laughers (*risores*) who are intermediate between serious honorable men and the brutes by representing them as satyrs.

[27] Hence mockers and scoffers (*derisores*) because of their perverting dispositions are always insincere and the riches of the divine truth are not available to them. Because they enjoy to make fun of things true and honorable, the words of Divine Wisdom apply to them (*Proverb*, 9:12): "If you are wise you are the one who will profit" and "If you are a mocker or scoffer (*derisor*) you are the cause of your ruin." This explanation of the nature of laughter explains also why funny personae in the comedies, the comics, are more effective when they tell foolish things in a serious manner, and equally are ineffective when they try to make the spectators laugh while they themselves are laughing. Truly, there is no more entertaining performance than when mimes imitate known serious and severe persons in their look, gestures, and actions, and by so doing ridicule them on stage. All of the above boiled down to this: laughter comes from the deceit set up for the human intellect that yearns for truth and therefore a person laughs more profusely as more impressive is the simulation of truth.

[28] Cicero quite correctly and elegantly said that laugh bursts from what is moderately disgraceful, and not from the truly wicked like something absolutely false, or the contrary of truth, or, even less, from what the schools call contradictory. Contradiction inflicts great pain to the mind and the mind reacts with indignation and rage because

natura, per omnes populos gentesque longe lateque diffusa et
per omnes aetates circumagente, constantiam desiderat iste se-
460   verus systematum censor et gravis qui, in ista brevi fabula quam
de me fingit, omni ex parte sibi non constat!

    [*34*] Principio enim illa quam inter se minime convenien-
tia? Neapolitanum auctorem novi systematis ad ingenium Romano-catholicae religionis accommodati suum inter Romano-
465   catholicos celare nomen, et systema Romano-catholicum universae Italorum catholico-romanae nationi esse taedio! An auctor
suum iccirco celavit nomen ne eo Italorum taedio opprimere-
tur? At enim novarum auctores doctrinarum viae ad opprimen-
dum patent omnino duae, nimirum quando ii suae rei publicae
470   aut religionem aut regimen novis doctrinis suis labefactant.

    [*35*] Deinde illa quam vix credibilia? Perexiguum duo-
decim, non amplius, foliorum libellum universam Italorum nationem ad taedium commovisse, et auctorem, qui gentiles suos
universos commovit, tam bene latere ut ipsius et praenomen
475   et status et ordo ignoretur!

    [*36*] Postremo quam illa sibi contraria? Nam cur univer-
sam Italorum nationem taedio is liber affecit? An quia multo
labore contra Grotii et Pufendorfii doctrinas et principia disputat? Sed nationum naturam id proprium certe consequitur,
480   ut qui cum fortissimis externarum nationum viris multo labore sive [8r] acriter pugnat, is, prae gloriae aemulatione,
genti suae plurimum afferat voluptatis eiusque universa in se
studia mirum in modum conciliet. An quia id argumentum ab
transalpinis iam satis superque sit celebratum; unde illa uber-
485   rima scriptorum seges: Grotii, Seldeni, Pufendorfii, eius doctrinae principes, Vandermuelenii, Barbeiracii, Boecleri, Zuicleri,
Grotii alii, Gronovii, Vitriarii, omnes Hugonis adornatores,
Buddaei, Zentgravii, Uberi, Thomasii et, praeter hos celebrio-
res, alii minoris notae quam plurimi? Sit ita sane. Sed, si hic
490   Vicus nomine, horum transalpinorum de iure naturali gentium

aware of wicked falsehood. Laugh, then, bursts from what is moderately disgraceful and therefore as the acute saying is about what appeared different but in the substance was the same, that is, a true thing under the appearance of falsehood, so the argute saying is about what appears the same, but then is discovered to be different, that is something false which presented itself as something true. From this comes the kind of unexpected laughing that, like when some ridiculous characters appeared on the stage and all spectators laugh, Divine Wisdom described as bursting from the mouth of the fools. Latin people have quite wisely said that the mind of the fool is unstable; he is always in conflict with himself and changes opinion daily, moving from extreme to extreme; he vacillates and then succumbs.[22] Nature has also proved through physical movements that this is in a sense true because we experienced that common people at the sight of someone else unexpectedly slipping, or skidding, and falling can hardly retain themselves from snickering.

---

[22] An analysis of the nature of the fool is given by Vico in the second inaugural oration. See *On Humanistic Education (Six Inaugural Oration, 1699–1707)* (Ithaca: Cornell University Press, 1993), pp. 15, 62–69.

[29] Knowing, therefore, that instability of mind is the source of foolishness, philosophy is precisely concerned about it and intends to strengthen the constancy of the wise. In addition, let me confess how very enjoyable are for the spectators those representations in which the characters are accurately drawn like in the ancient Atellan and Oscan plays of the Roman times, which today in Italian we call *favole burlesche*, burlesque fables. This kind of plays affords a pleasure suitable to the wise whose mind is always interested in what is uniform, convenient, and suitable. The intensity of this pleasure is comparable to that experienced by the spectators of a game of soccer, for example, when they see that the ball kicked by one player reaches another player of the same team for whom the ball was intended. Alas! Representations of this kind can be produced only by writers experts in moral philosophy. The other types of ridiculous representations amuse the immoderate and the unrestrained with a kind of pleasure that makes the sane of mind insane, whose laughing chokes right reasoning.

[30] This is the reason why Demosthenes, doubtlessly the acutest of all orators, always used an incomparable manner of talking with which he guided his listeners through the subject of the case and jumping from one subject to another that had apparently nothing to do with the original one. While the audience was wondering what

edissertatis, novam methodum solam concinnasset, tamen res
non erat ut tantum taedium in Italia universa commoveret,
hac praesertim aetate in qua, cum facilitati unice mos geratur,
soli novarum methodorum tituli libros suavissimos faciunt. Sed
495   is vobis id Vici plane novum de integro systema esse nuncia-
vit. Atqui crebra, usitata, senescentia satietatem, fastidium ac
taedium gignunt; omnia autem nova placere in vulgatissimo
proverbio est. Verum ignotus erro ait, potius quam systema,
id merum esse « figmentum ». Esto, quando nihil aeque ac
500   figmenta delectant, ubi sunt apta, decora sibique ex omni sui
parte convenientia. Heic iste ignotus erro iam me sibi teneri
putat, quia in eo figmento ego coniecturarum mole mihi ipse
deficiam. Qui isthaec dicit, qui in brevi fabella, quam de me
meoque libro fingit, quantum vidimus tantum omni ex parte
505   sibi non constat?

     [37]   Ubi nequeo satis mirari quantas iste ignotus erro
sui delicias faciat ac proinde quam sit iniquus! [8v] Is enim
suam istam fabulam credi vult et, quia credi vult, credi putat
in eo cuius ipse contrarium verum agit, eodem tempore quo
510   eam de me meoque libro fabulam comminisci non potest nisi
per id cuius ipse contrarium verum agit, et quod verum agit,
id vero est ipsi rerum naturae conveniens! Nam cur is a vobis
celari sedulo curat iis verbis « Italus quidam », nisi quia systema ad ingenium pontificiae Ecclesiae accommodatum impro-
515   bat quidam Italus? Itane iste delicatulus agit? Per quod ipse
absconditur, per eius contrarium credi vult me celari? Cur ge-
nerico Itali nomine per totam Italiam ignotus errat iisdem verbis
« Italus quidam », nonne metu ne cuias sit in Italia deprehenda-
tur, quia enim is ab animo sibi male conscio mordetur se toti
520   Italorum nationi esse odio, quia systema ad ingenium pontificiae

his words were leading up to, he would then find among the many new things mentioned one aspect, one reason that would deal with the subject of the original case, bringing it to its well-constructed peroration. With his acutest manner of talking he was throwing out in all refined diction those short enthymemes that like lightning were vehemently and unexpectedly falling on the audience.[23] For this reason, Longinus compared Demosthenes, known as the enthymematic orator, to the fulminating physical phenomenon. He learned this manner of elocution when he, for many years, was a disciple of Plato who, using the dialectic of Socrates, when discussing one subject was questioning about some other subject that appeared wholly different from the initial topic, but from which he derived a new sentence that dealt exactly with a new aspect of the same original topic. This art of questioning, or dialectic as the Greeks say, was invented by Socrates, the wisest of philosophers, with the proposal of cultivating the natural ingenuity of the Greeks, who exceeded all other nations of

---

[23] These remarks on Demosthenes should integrate all that Vico said about him in the *Art of Rhetoric*. See particularly from the *De Chriis* the following sketch: "Among the orators whose works have arrived to us from Antiquity, Demosthenes is the one so perfect that he seems to have been made exclusively for our own advantage. In fact, all of the others show an abundance of vacuous words left dangling. But Demosthenes alone is so rich in word and thought so well placed that he can be esteemed in the assemblies to be not just a man but a Counsel in its entirety when he speaks, and in private, not an advocate acting alone, but a presiding judge" (pp. 264–265).

Ecclesiae accommodatum vobis narrabat id taedio esse universae Italorum nationi? Itane mecum aequo iure agit? Per quod
is sentit se Italis esse odio, credi vult me Italis esse taedio? En
qui in pene infinito et maxime serioso systemate constantiam
525   desiderat, qui in brevissima fabula est tam sui dissidens, tam
a se diversus tamque sibi ipse contrarius!
     [*38*] (t) Sed, tot caussis Italici eius taedii in superiore
nota, aliud agente, enumeratis, iisque cunctis reiectis, et eius
caussam tamen subesse per ipsum saltem necesse est, iste igno-
530   tus erro dicat tandem: quae est? Dicit, verum invitus dicit;
namque ego ab ipso exculpo caussam quam dicit: quia is
liber non intelligitur. Cur igitur eam caussam reticuit? Cur
scripto mandare ipsum puduit, in quo tot vana de me fin-
gere, tot falsa de libro mentiri non dubitavit? Qui tantus
535   iste eum pudor incessit, qui scripto mandare quod is liber non
intelligitur magis pudendum [9r] sensit quam quae sunt mendacia, quae dixit de me meoque libro audacissima? Ego pro
ipso dicam: quia, cum in eo libro de humanitatis principiis
disseratur nihilque afferatur usquam quod non ex communi
540 omnium hominum sensu depromptum sit, is, si quam sentie-
bat taedii sui caussam proferret, ipse communem sensum se
non habere scripto profiteretur. Sed heic ego istius ignoti erronis pectus rimabor eiusque mentem animumque vobis atque
adeo omnibus ostendam.

this world. This man, Demosthenes, who excelled for his acuity, could never move audiences to laugh with his orations, and, if sometime he wanted to move them to laugh, he was so inept that he appeared ridiculous.

END OF THE DIGRESSION AND CONTINUATION
OF THE LEGAL CLAIM

[31] Let this anonymous vagabond now figure out how much ingenuity is contrary to truth, given that there is nothing equal to ingeniousness in its efforts for the achievement of truth. This I have underlined many times since our digression began precisely in order to illustrate the point that this vagabond, together with the believe of common folks, accepted as truth that eloquence is completely other thing than philosophy.

THE CONTRADICTIONS
[pars. 32–39, r–s]

[32] (r) How skillful a lover of truth is this individual who publicly and openly lies by saying that my book is *in octavo*,[24] that I hide my name to the erudite and am an

---

[24] The expressions *in octavo* or *in duodecimo* are technical words of the early printing art. *In octavo* is said of a book size of about 6 x 9 inches, determined by printing on *sheets* folded to form 8 *leaves* or 16 *pages*. *In duodecimo* is said of a book size of about 5 x 7 and 1/2 inches, determined by printing on *sheets* folded to form 12 *leaves* or 24 *pages*. In paragraph 35, Vico tells us that

abbé! As I think of all this and reflect upon it, I wonder more and more whether a bad habit not only would corrupt right human nature but also pervert it. An example is this unknown vagabond who must have been born, nurtured, grown up and confirmed in falsities and fickle thoughts. He has previously affirmed, referring to what he imagined about me, that my system is merely a figment, and now, in agreement with his lie about the format of my book, he suggests that I care for no truth. This wretched man shows himself to be a miserable exemplar of those prisoners who, as the divine Plato divinely narrated, lived in an underground den that had a mouth open toward the light that reached all along the den. If for a long time these wretched beings could only see the shadows of those things behind them that are projected on the wall of the den, once they are released, would they not erroneously judge that the things outside the den also are shadows?

[33] (s) Is that not amazing that this severe censor of systems has found some incoherence in my science of the common nature of all peoples, everywhere diffused through all nations, and embracing all ages? He is the one who, in

---

his book of 12 *sheets in duodecimo* was a small book. He meant to say that his book was made out of 12 sheets, every sheet giving 24 pages, for a total of 288 pages. The different description of the size of the book is an important argument in favor of Vico's legal claim that his adversary has not even seen the book in question and has described something else!

this story he has invented about me, fully contradicts himself!

[34] Which ones are his contradictions? He said that a Neapolitan author of a new system in full conformity with the nature of the Roman-Catholic religion has not revealed his name among the Roman Catholic people! He added that this system that conformed with the Roman-Catholic Church has been received by the universal Catholic-Roman nation of Italians with indifference! Is it possible that the author did not reveal his name so that the Italians would not censure him? Truly, there are only two ways that induce the right criticism of authors of new doctrines: when they with their new doctrines undermine the nature of the fatherland and religion, or the legitimate government.

[35] How credible are his other affirmations, you tell me. A small book in twelve sheets format (*in duodecimo*) has moved to tediousness the whole Italian nation! Its author who has caused such upheaval has hidden himself so well that his first name, gentry, and nationality have remained unknown!

[36] Why are these statements contradictory? Why has this small book moved to tediousness all of the Italians? Perhaps because its author with great diligence challenged the doctrines and the assumptions of Grotius and Pufendorf?

545   [*39*] Is, mente quot diximus falsis offusa, animo fastus tu-
mente, cum eius libri temere, et qua se daretur, aperti unam et
item alteram paginam legeret, nec quicquam intelligeret — nam
qui talis et cum tali habitu posset! — uti delicati solent, qui
quavis minima re incommoda graviter offenduntur, statim li-
550 brum aspernatus eum fastidivit, et, uti faciunt superbi, qui
suas in alios transferunt culpas, [9v] suam indocilitatem mihi
obscuritatis vitio vertit, et, uti hominibus vulgo mos est, qui
ex suo spectant omnes animos aliorum, suum ipsius taedium
universae nationi Italorum affinxit. Sed quid nos in tam perspi-
555 cua re argumentationes quaerimus aut capimus coniecturas, quando in Italia tanto doctissimorum optimorumque virorum plausu
is liber exceptus est, ut perquam exiguus libellus, qui argumentum pium, severum et grave complectitur, intra annum aut
paullo plus eo rarissimus factus, duobus aureis numis usque a
560 bibliopolis in ipsa auctoris patria venditus sit, et nunc Venetiis
praeclarissimi nobilitate et doctrina viri, comes Ioh. Articus
de Porcia, quem supra honoris caussa nominavi, reverendus
pater Carolus Lodoli, pro sereniss. Venetorum re publica librorum censor, et excellentiss. abbas Antonius Conti, ex ordine
565 senatorum amplissimo, Anglis, Batavis, vobis, Germani, ipsis
Gallisque per hospitia literarum gratia cum primis huius seculi
literatis viris inita inclytus, ii me sint diligentissime per literas
cohortati ut ibi luculentis literariis formis et Claudiana sive
regia charta eum librum cum meis adnotationibus commenta-
570 riisve recudendum mandarem, uti re ipsa eorum cohortationi-
bus auscultans mandavi? Cuius unius libri caussa, opinor, aliquot seu bibliopolae seu typographi Veneti, per Bernardinum

Impossible! He who with great courage faces and challenges the most eminent personalities of foreign nations complies with the proper nature of nations for reason of each nation's pride, and gives much pleasure to his country folks and, with the universal admiration of all nations, also provides many advantages to himself. Or is it because the argument of the book has already sufficiently and abundantly been discussed by authors beyond the Alps? Yes, there is a great number of these writers: Grotius, Selden, and Pufendorf, who are the princes of that doctrine; Wilhelm van der Muelen, Jean Barbeyrac, Johann Heinrich Boeckler, Gaspar Ziegler and all the other Grotians like Johann Friedrich Gronow and Philippe Reinhald Glaser; all the embellishers of Grotius like Johann Franz Bude, Johann Joachim Zentraw, Ulrich Hüber, Christian Thomas; and many others less famous than these.[25] All right! But

---

[25] [Wilhelm van der Muelen (Vandermuelenius, 17th century) wrote *Exercitationes in Titutlum Digestorum de Iustitia et Iure et Historiam Pomponii de Origine Iuris*. Jean Barbeyrac (Barbeyracius, 1674—1744) translated and commented the works of Grotius and Pufendorf. Johann Heinrich Boeckler (Boeclerius, 17th century) wrote *Institutiones Politicae* and *Dissertationes Politicae ad Selecta Veterum Historicorum Loca et Libellus Memorialis Ethicus* (1674). ... Philippe Reinhald Glaser (Vitriarius, 17th century) published *Universum Ius Civile Privatum ad Methodum Institutionum Iustiniani* (1697). Johann Franz Bude (Buddaeus, 1667—1729), a protestant theologian, wrote *Elementa Philosophiae Practicae* (1697). Johann Joachim Zentraw (Zentravius, 17th century) wrote *Disquisitio de Origine, Veritate et Obligatione Iuris Gentium* (1684). Ulrich Hüber (Uberius, 1636–1694) wrote *Digressiones Iustinianeae* (1671)

what would you say if this author by the name of Vico, after having discussed the doctrines on the natural law of the nations of these authors beyond the Alps, formulated a truly new method, would then the book cause boredom among all the Italians, especially in our time when the general custom is that of easily and uniquely publishing books with titles announcing new methods? Is it not true that the vagabond has acknowledged that Vico's book is about a new system? Is it not the most popular proverb saying that trite matters, known and common, generate boredom, fastidiousness, and tediousness, while new ones give pleasure? The vagabond said that mine is not a system but a true figment. Oh, I may accept that! There is nothing that gives equal pleasure as the figments that are suitably, decorously, and harmoniously composed. The anonymous vagabond thought of having crushed me by affirming that the enormous pile of my conjectures would bring my defeat by way of contradictions. Is he not the one who in the short fairy tale he narrated about me and my book fell into contradictions, as we saw?

[37] At this point I really cannot stop from wondering about how much satisfaction this unknown vagabond is

---

and *De Iure Civitatis* (1682). Christian Thomas (Thomasius, 1655—1728), a German, on the footsteps of Pufendorf wrote *Fundamenta Iuris Naturae ac Gentium ex Sensu Communi Deducta* (1705). Gaspar Ziegler (Zuiclerus, 17th century) wrote *Notae et Animadversiones*, that is, comments and discussions on the *De Iure Belli ac Pacis* of Grotius.]

having from all this and how much wicked he must be. He wants that his own story be believed and, because he wants it to be believed, he thinks that it should be believed as true though it is contrary to truth. But at the same time he cannot mix together that story about me and my book, unless he mixes together what is contrary to truth and what it is true, which has its confirmation in the reality of things! Why is he so careful in hiding his name by only revealing that he is *Italian*? Surely because how could an Italian otherwise criticize a system conforming with the doctrines of the Roman Church? Isn't he scrupulous? Does he wish to make us believe that I concealed my name [as he falsely affirmed] for the reason contrary to the one by which he concealed his own? Why is he traveling unknown throughout Italy and only introducing himself with the generic name of *an Italian*? Is he afraid that his own place of origin in Italy would become known? He surely is aware of having lied and is afraid of being hated by the Italians for having claimed that a system in conformity with the doctrines of the Roman Church moved Italian people to boredom and tediousness! Is he not treating me in an equal manner? Does he want you to believe that the reason why Italians hate him is the same reason why they dislike my book?

Gessarium bibliopolam et Felicem Mosca typographum, Neapolitanum utrumque, a me petiere ut libros omnes, quos in
575 « Catalogo » subnexo meae « Vitae » indicatos superius dixi,
ad ipsos mitterem, quos, in unum corpus compositos, literariis
typis recuderent. Quod utrique, gratia iis Venetis pro officio
habita, denegavi, qui unum hunc, de quo [10r] vobiscum
nunc ago, librum, de omnibus quos scripsi, superesse, si per
580 rerum naturam fieri posset, exoptarem.

NOTARUM CONCLUSIO

[*40*] Igitur, ut hanc rem totam complectar et vobis ad
exitum tandem perducam, vehementer suspicor, et, ob haec
quae omnia concurrunt simul, firmissimam coniecturam hanc
585 facio, ex qua iste ignotus erro in re sua experiatur an ego mea
coniecturarum mole mihi ipse deficiam.
[*41*] Iste relator « Novae Scientiae » proprium subiectum
silentio praeteriit; libri formam 8° meque meum in eo libro
eruditos celare nomen mentitus est; meum statum finxit; meum
590 ordinem et, ubi me vobis privatim nominat, meum praenomen tacuit; primarium eius Scientiae subiectum de iure naturali gentium esse simulavit; me contra Seldenum, alium a
Grotio et Pufendorfio, eius doctrinae principem, disputare
transmisit; idque systema figmentum esse perperam dixit, ne-
595 que ex veritate Romano-catholicae Ecclesiae profectum, sed ad
ingenium pontificiae Ecclesiae accommodatum esse inique cen-
suit, et quod in eo magis ingenio quam veritati indulgeam
absurde iudicavit; tandem, in eo uno iste sui semper similis,
perpetuo nempe mendacio, uti incoeperat et perrexerat, ita

Oh! This is the same guy who could not find coherence in a system almost infinite and greatly important and who in his shortest tale [about me and my book] is so fragmented and inconsistent to fall into an absolute contradiction![26]

---

[26] [The hidden references to the accusations and process brought against the Neapolitan "atheists" touched so many friends of Vico that one wonders how he could escape that kind of persecution. This process had been openly opposed by the Viceroy of Naples Bonavides, and more cautiously by his successor, the Duque of Medinaceli, who used to frequent the Academy of Caravita, that is, the academy of the anticurialists of Naples. In 1696, Vico wrote an eulogy for Bonavides and in 1697 wrote an epicedium at the death of the mother of the Duque, Caterina of Aragon. Vico must have been a confessed anticurialist as well at that time or at least a friend of the anticurialists, sharing their ideals and programs. The "unknown vagabond" is now accusing him. Why? He believes that Vico who in his youth must have share the doctrines of the anticurialists with Costantino Grimaldi and Pietro Giannone, has now abandoned anticurialism and separated himself from its supporters. In other words, Vico has become a friend of priests and monks, and has expressed in his "first new science" a new system of natural law or rather a fable on the natural law ... in the taste of the Church of Rome. Naturally, Vico reacted vehemently. He is a Catholic believer, a friend of members of the priesthood and religious orders, but this does not preclude that he still holds previous convictions, the ones he held when he frequented the academy of Caravita. The conception of the natural law of nations that Vico exposed in the *First New Science* is certainly common to the Church of Rome for the reason that it springs from the common nature of nations. ... The unknown vagabond has removed himself from the Catholic Church and has embraced Protestantism. The proof of this is that the vagabond uses typical arguments used by Lutheranism. ... The same argument was used by the Protestant philologist Jacobus Perizonius against the Catholic Franciscus Sanchez, author of *Minerva seu de Causis Linguae Latinae*. ... This was exactly what Vico has done: he accepted the interpretation of the Gospel according to the principles established by the Council of Trent and not according to the Word Itself of the Divine Gospel.

[38] (t) In the above comments all the reasons of the Italian boredom have been enumerated and all have been confuted. But there was necessarily a concealed reason behind them, a reason that this unknown vagabond should finally reveal to us. Which is it? He is unaware of having already told us. I discovered it between the lines of his review of the book: "this book is unintelligible!" Why did he not explicitly say so? Why on one hand was he afraid to publicly say that, when on the other hand he fantasized many things about me and dared to publicly say many false ones about the book? Did he feel more embarrassed to say that the book was unintelligible than to concoct all those outrageous lies about me and the book? I will answer for him. Given that the book deals with the principles of humanity and all arguments in it are derived from the common sense of all human beings, if he had explicitly explained the cause of the tediousness, he would have to

---

... In his book he has certainly exposed a conception that did not offend the convictions of the Catholic Church ... he has not exposed the doctrine of the Catholic Church but a conception in harmony with the religious vision of life common to all the Italian nation. This conception is also common to the Church of the Popes but only because it derives from the common nature of nations. For this reason, Vico had no need to hide his name that he instead clearly stated more than once at the beginning of his book. In contrast to the unknown vagabond, Vico had no need to hide who he was, where he lived, whence he came. ... In Naples, the best men can be unticurialist and at the same time profoundly religious. Anticurialism is one thing and the Catholic Roman religiosity another. ... In the *Vici Vindiciae*, Vico reaffirms the coherence, the autonomy, and the profound religiousness of his thought.]

600 falso clausit relationem, quod is liber ab universa Italorum
natione cum taedio exceptus est. Quae, sub una mihi praeclara
exceptione, sunt numero illa omnia falsa quae initio vobis
proposui in vestra « Eruditorum Acta » de me meoque libro
relata esse. Iste, inquam, relator vobis haec omnia retulit,
605 quia, una excogitatae malitiae opera, voluit effecta reddere
haec quinque: primum, ut [10v] meam dignitatem laederet;
secundum, ut vos eius libri inquirendi negligentes faceret; ter-
tium, ut, si eum diligentius perquirere velletis, difficilem vobis eius copiam efficeret; quartum, ut, si maxime eum alicubi
610 nacti fuissetis, alium putaretis librum, auctorem alium; quinc-
tum et postremum, ut is interea in atra nocte tot tantarumque
fraudum lateret et vos eum fidum amicum putare pergeretis:
ex quibus effectis quinque, is, uno, meum apud vos nomen
obscuraret; tribus, apud omnes ad quos is liber per Europam
615 penetravit nomen vestrum minueret; uno reliquo, in quo uno
ei spes impunitatis affulserat, sui nominis obscuritati caveret.
    [42] Sed, ut initio tria persequar quae ad vos attinent
— nam primum ad me spectare videtur, postremum ad ipsum
re vera pertinet — quaerentibus vobis librum 8° cui titulus
620 « Principi d'una Scienza nuova del diritto naturale delle genti »,
auctoris anonymi, bibliopola certe responderet se eum librum
anonymi auctoris, cuius is titulus et forma sit, ignorare planissime. Deinde, edentibus vobis illa argumenta seu signa:
quanquam eius libri auctor nomen suum eruditos celet, certio-
625 res tamen facti sumus a quodam nostro amico Italo ipsum esse
abbatem Neapolitanum cui nomen Vici sit, bibliopola, maxime
si eum librum perquireretis Neapoli, ubi me neque caelibem
esse neque orbum omnes norunt, procul dubio diceret se hunc
hominem Neapolitanum eius libri auctorem non nosse; scire

confess in writing that he has no common sense. I should therefore pry into the heart, the mind, and the spirit of this unknown vagabond and show you [what kind of man he is].

[39] This person, whose mind is overcome by falsehood as we said, and whose spirit is swollen with arrogance, must indifferently have opened the book and read one and then another page at random, and did not understand it. How could a person such as he understand it? Like the persons who seriously reject a book when they find it not to their taste from reading a few pages at random, he disliked it. Like the arrogant who never recognizes his mistakes, he excused his inability of understanding with the lack of clarity in my writing. Like the vulgar folks who think that their own opinion is the common opinion of all others, he reflected his own tediousness on the whole Italian nation. In a matter so evident, why should I use arguments and conjectures, when some of the most learned and respectable persons have praised this book? Within a year or little more from its publication, this small book that deals with important, pious, and severe matter has become so rare that, in the city of the author, bookstores sold it at two golden liras the copy. Men of learning and prestige like Giovanni Artico da Porcia, whom I respectfully already mentioned, the Reverend Father Carlo Lodoli, Books Reviewer for the Republic of Venice, and the Honorable

Antonio Conti of the Senate of the Republic, famous among the English, the French, and you, O German gentlemen, and highly estimated by the most illustrious literati of our age, have written to me. From Venice, they have kindly precisely requested that I send them a copy of the book with my notes and comments, saying that they would print it this time on special paper and in an elegant format. It was a thing to which I felt honorably obliged. Motivated by the good fortune of the book some Venetian booksellers or printers, through the mediation of Bernardino Gessari, a bookseller, and Felice Mosca, a printer, both of Naples, requested that I put together all the writings I listed in the appendix to my *Autobiography* and send the whole corpus to them so that it will be published in a new edition. I properly thanked the Venetian gentlemen, but I did not what Gessari and Mosca asked me to do, because I would wish, if human possible, that of all the books written by me, this one alone, the book I now discuss with you, would be my only work to remain.

630 tamen Neapolitanum eius nominis esse Ioh. Baptistam Vicum,
qui maritus et pater est et auctor libri, non 8° sed 12°, cuius
titulus est: « Principi d'una Scienza nuova dintorno alla natura delle nazioni ». Postremo, vobis omnes libros luculentio-
ris argumenti [11r] vel celebrioris auctoris pro munere vestro
635 conquirentibus rogantibusque ut idem bibliopola, et, nisi is,
qui ' forte fortuna ' alius eum in bibliotheca apud se habens,
eius vobis copiam faceret, isque, pro raritate tam brevi tempore, quantum diximus, facta, eum vobis perquam caro ven-
didisset, vos, cum legeretis eius Scientiae proprium subiectum
640 esse de communi nationum natura, ex qua apud omnes populos aeque manat notitia de divinarum rerum humanarumque
originibus, unde postremo profluit novum de iure naturali gentium systema, quod non contra Grotium et Pufendorfium solos
sed etiam contra Seldenum, alium eius doctrinae principem,
645 stabilitur, idque pontificiae Ecclesiae cum genere humano universo commune esse; cum, quemadmodum mihi persuadeo, id
observaretis constabilitum genere disserendi cum veritate et
constantia, cumque postremo eum librum, pro parva ipsius
mole et editione nimis recenti, perquam caro emissetis et,
650 quando precii caritas est optimarum exoptatarumque mercium
potissimum argumentum, intellexissetis eum librum Italis esse
percharum; ob haec omnia vos certe, quidem hercule, eum
librum putaretis omnino alium ab eo quem iste ignotus erro
vobis narravit. Cumque ibi, a meo praenomine admoniti, agnos-
655 setis me esse ipsissimum illum Ioh. Baptistam Vicum de quo
dominus Clericus, de aliis meis libris, quos supra memoravi,
super eo ipso argumento quanquam exasciato, honorificentis-
sime verba facit, et eum exponeretis verius et de eo censeretis
aequius et de me loqueremini forsan magis cum dignitate.
660   [43] [11v] Iam istud a vobis, eruditi viri Lipsienses, factum mihi vobiscum his « Notis » transactum est. Nunc autem su-
perest seorsim caussa de qua cum isto ignoto errone, qui id

CONCLUSION OF THESE NOTES
[pars. 40–43, t]

[40] In order to bring this whole matter to an end I firmly claim that, having considered all things, it is reasonable to infer that this unknown vagabond will finally come to know if I contradicted myself because of the extensive number of conjectures in the book.

[41] As the reviewer of the book, he has not even mentioned the precise argument of *The First New Science*. He has lied about the format of the book and my last name. He has invented my civil status and kept quiet about my profession and when he mentioned me to you, he never revealed my first name. He [erroneously] suggested that the primary matter dealt by *The First New Science* is the natural law of nations and did not tell that I discussed with Selden, a prince of that doctrine who held a different opinion than Grotius and Pufendorf. He affirmed that the system herein presented is a pure figment and unfairly judged that, though it is not derived from the truth of the Roman-Catholic Church, it is still acceptable to the Church of Rome. He absurdly pronounced that in that work I complied more with ingenuity than truth. He was however coherent in lying at the end as he did in the beginning, when he concluded his review saying that this book was received by the whole Italian nation with tediousmess and indifference. In my defense, as I stated it at the beginning,

vobis extra ordinem retulit et super eo sententiae loco dixit, quaedam familiariter loquar.

665 ## AD IGNOTUM ERRONEM ADMONITIO

[44] Dic mihi, bone vir, si, in imo tuae civitatis ordine et loco positus, quidam e spurca plebe homo esses atque istius modi flagitia in vili pecunia faceres ut eam domino auferres, numnam scis te stellionatus crimine damnatum ignominiosa
670 poena plecti oportere? Agesis, si ea poena te maneret ubi isthaec in vili pecunia deliquisses, quo longe graviore te supplicio dignum esse fatearis necesse est qui isthaec ipsa, quantum abs te in te et per te fuit, admisisti in dignitate atque existimatione honesti viri Neapolitani de te nihil male meriti,
675 ut qui totam sic vitam peregit ut coluerit omnes, iuverit multos, laeserit neminem, et, quanquam ab adversa fortuna conflictatus et quia conflictatus, ut suam adversam fortunam solaretur, ab sapientiae studiis mutuatus solamina, tamen pro sua infirma virili parte, nedum Neapolitani sed universi Italici
680 nominis amplitudini et Ecclesiae Romano-catholicae gloriae multo labore et summa industria studuit, et inter Italos hanc de iure naturali gentium praeclarissimam provinciam, in qua literati viri transalpini et soli et maxime summi et toti fervent, primus omnium adornare, idque religioni Romano-catholicae
685 consonum, non Italorum modo sed omnium prorsus primus, statuminare conatus est? Nonne satis graviter deliquisses,

so I again declare that all these things that have been said about me and my book in your *Acta Eruditorum* are false. Let me be clear. This reviewer has referred to you all these things with the intentional wicked plan of achieving these five goals. First, he wished to tarnish my dignity; second, he wanted to divert you from paying careful attention to the book; third, in the case you intended to make a diligent search, he wanted to make difficult the finding of a copy of the book; fourth, if you could ever find a copy, he wanted that you believe that it was a different book of a different author; fifth, though in that tenebrous night of lies, he wanted you to continue to consider him as a trustworthy friend. Of these five aims one was to obscure my name to you, three were to tarnish your name before all the people of Europe in whose hands this book has arrived, and in the last one he assured his impunity by keeping his name in the darkness.

[42] Let's begin with the three aims that relate to you since the first concerns me and the last one the unknown vagabond. If you were to ask a bookseller about a book *in octavo* whose title is *Princípi d'una Scienza Nuova del Diritto Naturale delle Genti* of an anonymous author, he would clearly answer that he has no knowledge about an anonymous author of a book in that format and with that title. If thereafter you were willing to give more information to the bookstore saying that though the author kept his

[12r] si esses Romano-catholicus? si Italus, longe gravius?
si Neapolitanus, gravissime? Sed ista in me tua, ignotus erro,
seu dicta seu facta omitto, quae mox senties in me nec facta
690 nec dicta esse.

[*45*] Quid autem illa quibus tot ac tales literatos Lipsien-
sis collegii viros, qui universam literariam rem publicam, suis
« Eruditorum Actis » tantopere collatis operis, iuvare conni-
tuntur, qui te sibi sanctissimo amicitiae vinculo coniunctum
695 praedicant, « amicus noster Italus », qui suam dignitatem atque
existimationem tuae diligentiae atque integritati committunt,
qui tuam fidem tanta fiducia sequuntur ut, tanquam in tua
verba iurati, quae tu illis falsissima narras ii in se ipsi vera
recipiant et suo ipsorum nomine ea pro veris toti Europae
700 eruditae edicere et provulgare non dubitent; tu sic eos cir-
cumvenis, decipis, prodis, ut de eodem libro eodemque auctore, [12v] tanquam de rebus et personis omnino aliis, prorsus contraria scriberent — quod sane quoddam monstri simile
est — neque te peccati sui esse auctorem rescire possent, illa
705 sua Germana fide rati te ipsis de alio libro, de alio auctore
retulisse? Nisi si id est, quod tu factitas, per Deum immor-
talem, quid est amicitiam de humanis rebus tollere, fidem e ci-
vili hominum vita eiicere, atque adeo funditus evertere hu-
manam societatem?
710 [*46*] Fortasse inquies hanc eius libri inquirendi negligen-

name hidden to the public, nonetheless an Italian friend of yours has assured you that he is a Neapolitan priest whose last name is Vico, then the bookseller—especially if you were to look for this book in Naples where everybody knows that I am neither celibate nor childless—would without reticence reply that he does not know this Neapolitan man author of such a book. He would nonetheless confess that he knows a Neapolitan whose name is Giambattista Vico, married and with children, author of a book *in duodecimo* whose title is *Princípi d'una Scienza Nuova dintorno alla Natura delle Nazioni*. Then again if you were, as it is your duty, to inquire about more important books of more famous authors and asked the same bookseller or some other whether they may have on the shelves of the store a copy of this book, you would have to pay dearly because in a brief time after publication it has become rare. Reading the book, you will discover that its proper argument is the common nature of nations, from which among all peoples equally originates the awareness of the origins of divine and human things, from which then a new system of the natural law of nations is built. This new system of the natural law of nations refutes Grotius and Pufendorf, but also Selden, the third prince of that doctrine, and is common to the Church of Rome and the whole humankind.

tiam, hanc eius potiundi difficultatem, hunc de alio libro alio-
que auctore errorem, in quae tu, Vice, dicis me Lipsienses literatos inducere voluisse, eas caussas tres ipsis cum omnibus
Europae literatis viris esse communes, ac proinde iis ipsorum
715   esse salvam dignitatem. At enim isthinc, nec aliunde, perspicue significas quam ab iniusta rabie mentem offusam habeas,
qui non vides ut, quod contra me egisse putas, id re ipsa sit
plane nihil; namque ista, quam dicis pro te, caussa mihi ɛ
Lipsiensibus literatis individua est; cumque liber, meus genui-
720   nus partus, iam per totam Italiam vulgatus sit et Alpes quoque
etiam superarit et mare traiecerit, apud quosnam literatos Europae viros tu dignitatem laesisti meam? An gloriam nominis
in eo stare putas, ut ii ad quos alicuius viri fama sit pervagata,
illi eius faciem, vultum, colorem, staturam habitumque con-
725   spiciant? O inclyti gloria viri, aut iamdiu defuncti aut nimium
longinqui, qui nominis claritudinem vobis virtute, doctrina
sapientiaque comparastis, nulli per istum vos estis quia po-
steris, exteris, corpora vestra haudquaquam conspecta sunt!
     [47] [13r] Si igitur apud eos omnes qui istum alium librum,
730   istum auctorem alium esse falso opinantur, tu meam dignitatem non laeseras, certe apud eos laedere voluisti qui istum
librum, auctorem istum in rerum natura non esse certo sciunt.
Quinam ii sunt nisi uni docti viri Neapolitani? Igitur tuum

111

I am convinced that—having found that this small book is solidly established on arguments of truth and coherence and having paid dearly because new and already rare, given that high prices are an indication of the best and most desired goods—you will understand how dear this book has been to Italians. By Hercules, from all this you should be able to see how different this book is from the one that the unknown vagabond has made you to believe. By knowing my first name, you should recognize me as that same Giambattista Vico about whom the Honorable Le Clerc, speaking about various other books of mine, which I mentioned above on the same argument, though in a summary way, pronounced praiseworthy words. I am confident that finally you would speak more truly about the book and review it more equitably, perhaps even referring to me in a more respectful manner.

[43] This is what we, you and I, have done so far, O learned gentlemen of Leipzig, with this transaction and my notes. Now with the remaining part of my case I must address the unknown vagabond who informed you improperly and unjustly, and I will speak with him in friendly terms.

ADMONITION TO THE ANONYMOUS VAGABOND
[pars. 44–50]

[44] Tell me, O my good man, if you were a common folk of the lower class in your society and in the business of handling vile money were to steal from the person over you, would you not be charged with the crime of fraud and condemned to a shameful punishment? Do you follow me? If you would be punished for a fraud regarding some vile money, would you not confess of deserving a greater punishment if you directly and intentionally planned and perpetrated the same in regard to the dignity and the uprightness of a honest Neapolitan citizen who never did anything to offend you? In whole his life this person has respected all human beings, helped many, and hurt no one. Touched by misfortune, in order to find some comfort for himself, he embraced the studies of wisdom, and according to his minimal ability he contributed to the fame of the name of Naples and of all Italians and to the glory of the Roman Catholic Church with great dedication and hard work. He was the first Italian who contributed in the excellent field of studies on the natural law of nations, a field in which all the learned scholars of beyond the Alps were alone supreme and greatly shining.

735 privatum, erro, in me odium in universos doctos viros Neapolitanos evomis et diffundis, quos tu gentibus cunctis diblateras libri veram religionem, quam profitentur, regiamque politiam, qua reguntur, adprobantis taedere et popularem Lipsiensium affectare libertatem? Porro incredibilem animi tui perversitatem considera, qui id egisti, ut non solum eo quod concupisti fru-

740 stratus abires, sed id ipsum multo acrius te ureret invidia, qua macescis. Namque, [13v] ut hominem, qui nusquam est, ab literatis Lipsiensibus inhoneste acceptum esse divulgares, cum vano isto eius libri, qui etiam quoque nusquam est, Italico taedio, hunc mihi gloriae locum fecisti luculentissimum, quod mea

745 privata haec caussa ita agglutinaretur et patriae pietati et Italiae decori et religionis Romano-catholicae sanctitati, ut mea et illarum una esset eademque defensio! Sed haec omnia sint, quae dico, tam falsa quam sunt plane verissima, non cogitasti — quod cuivis in mentem veniret — siqua hinc Neapoli ad

750 Lipsienses literatos viros manasset [14r] istum librum, aucto-

Of all Italians and even of all mankind he was the first who put all his efforts in building a system [of the natural law of nations] consonant with the Roman catholic religion.[27] [Would you not confess to deserve a greater punishment if you directly and intentionally planned and perpetrated the same in regard to the dignity and the uprightness of this person?] Would you not have transgressed seriously if you were Catholic; far more seriously, if you were Italian; most seriously if a Neapolitan? O unknown vagabond, I dismiss these words and facts against me because soon you will hear why they have not been said or done against me.[28]

[45] Are you aware that your words truly wounded many scholarly gentlemen of the great community of

---

[27] Vico lists his accomplishments not for personal pride, but as the necessary counter arguments against the slandering vagabond. Among the Italians of the eighteenth century Vico was indeed the first to become accepted and valued in the fields of philology, jurisprudence, and history. Jean Le Clerck made this fact public in his journal, *Bibliothéque Ancienne et Moderne*. See *Autobiography*, pp. 158 159, and *Universal Right*, p. 724.

[28] 27. A comparative study of *The Art of Rhetoric* and the *Vici Vindiciae* would show how Vico followed in all its part the different stages of how to develop a legal argument of defense as they are structure in the great manual of the *Institutiones Oratoriae*. Though Vico's case is purely demonstrative and not judicial, nonetheless he has presented at first the selection of loci (*Vici Vindiciae*, pars. [2]; *The Art of Rhetoric*, ch. 23), then the disposition (pars. [3]; ch. 24), the exordium (dedication and pars. [4–8]; ch. 25), the narration (pars. [9–19]; ch. 26), the digression (pars. 20–31; ch. 27), the proposition (pars. [32–39]; ch. 28), the division (pars. [2] and [38]; ch. 29), the confirmation (included in pars. [32–39]; ch. 30), the amplification (pars. [40–43]; ch. 31), the confutation (pars. [44–50]; ch. 32), and the peroration (pars. [51–52]; ch. 33).

Leipzig, who with the publication of notices of important works in the *Acta Eruditorum* aim at supporting the universal Republic of Letters? They confessed that you are a part of their society through the sacred bond of friendship. They spoke of you as their Italian friend, committed their honor and fame to your diligence and integrity, and placed total trust in you, ready to swear on your words. You, however, gave them words that were the falsest, which they accepted as true and did not refrain from making them known to all Europe in their name as true. You have deceived, mislead, swindled them in such a manner that they would dare to write about the same book and the same author as of persons and things completely different, even contrary, like something monstrous, without being capable of suspecting that you were the source of their blunder. In their German good faith they thought you gave them information about another book and author. [Because they could not have not known about my name and book!]. O God Immortal, is this not what you have been doing? Is not your doing the riddance of friendship among human beings? An elimination of trust within the civil society of humankind? And all the more the uprooting of human society from its foundation?

rem istum Neapolitanum nec extare nec unquam extitisse, quid
animi illis futurum esset, quam impense ipsos suae in te lo-
catae fiduciae poeniteret, quam graviter suam satis bonam fidem
incusarent, quam animitus suam amicitiam a te proditam esse
755 quererentur? Forsan ad haec illud semper turpe dictu respon-
deas, quod qui se ignorantia defendunt solent dicere: « Non
putabam eos laedere, qui laedere te unum volebam ». Et id
non sat tibi fuit ut haec cogitares: primum, quod, ut me
adgredereris, universi eius literatorum hominum collegii aucto-
760 ritate senseras te armari oportere; deinde, quod eius collegii
universi, non tua ignoti erronis, de eo libro iusta relatio erat
— nam iustam censuram integra ab omni ambitione obibit
temporis futuri longinquitas — postremo, quod est gravissi-
mum, quod, ut me, quem sive Italici nominis invidia sive re-
765 ligionis Romano-catholicae odium hostem tuum tibi confinxerat,
ne levi quidem ictu perstringeres, per tot tuos amicos gladium
infestum in me intenderes et in tot, quot transverberasti, literatis viris totum ferrum exhaurires?

    [*48*] [*14v*] Vide in quo abrupto ac praecipiti loco stes,
770 ut tuorum gravissimorum criminum a criminibus longe gravio-
ribus defensionem implores! Nam isthaec, non crudelitas sed

[46] You may perhaps reply, "O Vico, the negligence in reviewing a book, the difficulty in locating it, the misinformation about it and its author that you say I perpetrated in regard to the literati of Leipzig are truly three reasons for errors common not to them alone but to all literati of Europe, and thus I know that their respectability remained untouched." Well! In that case you would perspicuously have shown the unjust fury that blinded your mind, because you cannot see that what you did to me was truly grave. These words in your defense are turning into a favorable case for me and the literati of Leipzig. Yes, since my book, my genuine offspring, was already diffused everywhere throughout Italy, across the Alps and the sea, may I ask which literati of Europe have you convinced of my ineptness? Do you think that the glory of a good name when the fame of a man has arrived among some peoples consists in the notice about the characteristics of his look, countenance, color, height, and attire? O illustrious men of glory, already deceased or living in far away places, who made your name famous with virtue, doctrine, and wisdom, for this vagabond you are nothing because the generations after you and those living in far away places when you lived could never have seen or would never see your features and your other physical characteristics!

vecors immanitas esset appellanda, si vel iustus miles, nihil pensi habens civium pietatem — ex qua qui civem in praelio ab hoste servasset civica corona donabatur — is, aestuante conflictu,

775 per commilitonis corpus hostem confoderet. Quid tu qui, ociose meditatus, ut idem ipsum facere, officium, fidem, amicitiam nihil pensi habuisti? An id esse in corporibus nefas, in mentibus vero animisque, per quae homines sumus, putas ludum iocumque? Sed vide uti tua invidi rabies te caeco furore agitat

780 ac divexat, qui, ut me, tuo infensissimo odio destinatum, caedas, scutum, quod te protegit, pertundis ac perforas, et me tute ipse statuis extra ictum, qui de alio libro, de alio auctore retulisti; qui cum in rerum natura non sint, tu certe furis, qui umbras diverberas et vere tibi hostem finxisti quem ferires.

785 [49] Cum igitur talis sis, nempe [15r,3] in densis nominis tui tenebris vanus, et publicam hominum lucem aspicere non sustineas; amicis, inimicis aeque noxius; a tua patria, persequente nemine, aufugias; locum ubi, sive citra sive trans

[47] If you, therefore, have not injured my good name among all those who erroneously believe that the book is not mine but of another author, you certainly wished to hurt me nonetheless among those who certainly know that the book and the author that you have described in reality do not exist. And who are these peoples if not the learned Neapolitan gentlemen alone? Have you not heaved and diffused your personal hate for me over all the Neapolitan literati, about whom you prated to all nations that they remained indifferent to the book that endorses the true religion that they profess, the monarchic government by which they are ruled, and that instead they aspire at the popular liberty enjoyed by the literati of Leipzig? Oh the unbelievable perversity of your soul! Consider the consequence of what you did. The evil you intended for others fell on you and increased the burning envy that grows in you. You have publicized that an inexistent man has been unfairly estimated by the literati of Leipzig with a book of his that also did not exist but nonetheless motivated a universal Italian apathy for it. This in reality offered me a favorable opportunity for glory, because my personal case became so fused together with the respect for the fatherland, the honor due to Italy, and the sanctity of the Roman Catholic religion that their and my legal cause [against you and the *Acta*] would be one and the same! Let us admit that what I said may be false or true,

but allow me to ask if you have ever thought—what could have been very natural to anyone to do—about the consequences of your words and acts if from Naples scholars would have informed those of Leipzig that the precise book and the precise Neapolitan author do not exist and never existed? Can you imagine how the Leipzig's literati would have felt? Would they not have greatly regretted their trust in you and seriously accused themselves of excessive good faith? Would they not have animatedly charged you for betraying their friendship? To all these questions you may perhaps answer with the ludicrous saying of those who wish to excuse their faults by reason of ignorance: "I did not mean to hurt them but you!" Alright! But this was not enough to make you reflect on your misdeeds. With the purpose of attacking me, did you not feel necessary to shield yourself beforehand with the authority of the whole consortium of literati? In this way, O unknown vagabond, have you not assured that the right review of the book appeared to be theirs and not yours, though only in the progress of time the review will be just and totally immune from factitious drives? Finally, was this not the worst of your acts, when in order to hurt me whom you considered your enemy for your jealousy of the Italian name or your hate of the Roman Catholic religion, to transfix me you had to use your sword also against as many literati as you did?

121

[48] You are walking on the razor's edge because in order to defend your grave crimes you incur into some far more serious ones! Your deeds are due not to cruelty but to insane barbarism! Is it not true that by saving civilians from the enemy, soldiers deserve civic honors? But you like a military who disregards the respect due to civilians in the midst of the conflict, you killed an enemy piercing through the body of one of your own countryman. Is this not what you did when in your free planning you decided to discount responsibility, trust, and friendship? Do you think that the injuries inflicted on the body constitute a crime while those touching our mind and spirit, which are the ones that make us humans, are merely a game or a joke? Are you aware that your outrageous envy toward me blinded and possessed you in such a way that in your fury, through the shield that protects, you pierced shadows, leaving me safe and uninjured? Why? Because you gave information about another book and another author. In reality they do not exist. In your madness you strike phantasms, enemies that you fabricated.

[49] That is what you are: a vain shadow locked within your tenebrous and thick anonymity, which cannot sustains the common light enjoyed by all men. You are equally unwelcome to friends and enemies and, though there is no persecution, you run away from your own country. On both sides of the Alps, there is no place for you where to rest.

790 Alpes, consistas non habeas; cumque doctrina et eruditio, uti
bonae indolis homines meliores, ita malae quam deterrimos
faciant, ob haec omnia sedulo te hortor et moneo ut eruditi
nomen abs te abigas et, quantum fieri potest, amoveas: nam
satius est rudem esse cum innocentia quam, cum tanta noxia
ignotum, generis humani extorrem, quamvis doctissimum, per-
795 errare.

[*50*] [15v,15] Iam tandem vobis, Lipsienses literati viri,
eius libri legendi, quam iste relatione sua fecerat negligentiam
ego his « Notis » feci necessitatem, ex quibus, ne per hunc
erronem vos quoque erretis diutius, quando nullum eius apud
800 me exemplum extat, donec Venetiis recusus ad vos portetur,
interea me in eo libro hoc disserendi genere uti resciscatis, atque
inde coniectetis, quod his « Notis » egomet mei adsertor, me
verum eius veri libri auctorem esse aio, et illum Vicum nomine, quem erro iste a me alienavit, me esse vindico: unde in
805 libri vestibulo « Vici Vindiciae » inscriptae sunt.

Doctrine and erudition make men of good character better than they are; but the wicked ones become absolutely perverse. For this reason I advice you to give up as promptly as possible your fame as a scholar, reminding you that it is preferable to be uncouth and honest than to be an unknown great scholar, rejected by humanity for his great crimes.

[50] Finally, O great literati of Leipzig, I have created with my notes the need for you to read the book that you have neglected when you received information from the unknown vagabond. I wish that you no longer remain in error about this book of which I don't possess any copy until it would be reprinted in Venice, from where a copy would be sent to you. In the meantime I confirm that the book deals with the arguments I commented on in these notes, that I am the true author of that true book, and that Vico is my true name, name that this vagabond did not announce, though it is printed in the beginning of the book *Vici Vindiciae* (Vico's Legal Claim).

MY REQUEST TO THE IMPARTIAL READER

[pars. 51–52]

[51] O you who will calmly and impartially consider this series of notes, you should know that I wrote this opuscule in my room beside a humidifying device because of the lethal and progressive affliction [of my throat], for which the remedy is dangerous and apt to produce apoplexy in an elderly individual. Allow me to tell you more about this, since I spent almost twenty years researching the natural law of nations with the hope of coming up with some personal new contribution. To this end I spent most of my time hiding in a corner of the most isolated and respectful of silence library, a library on the contrary the richest in authors on the development of human thought, the richest in the most ancient authors of all nations, from whom a thousand years later the modern writers took their beginning. Thomas Hobbes also did as I, and he among all his literati friends and peers praised himself for being the first to meditate on this doctrine and contribute to its growth. In vain, however, he claimed all this, because he erroneously neglected to meditate on divine providence which alone can bring light to anyone searching for the origins of human institutions. Consequently, he lost himself within the most obscure and deplorable night of ancient history with the blind fate of Epicurus, against whose doctrine and principles I discuss in the first sections of my

book. For having done this, Jean Le Clerc in his yearly *Bibliothéque Ancienne et Moderne* praised me, and I regret to have forgotten to mention this in the comment marked with the letter (k) [13] in which this matter is dealt with. The unknown vagabond maliciously kept silent on this since it was to his advantage and did not wish to indicate the principles from which those he calls philosophers usually derived their systems of the natural law of nations. Among them we may count Pufendorf, but he must be purged because he was touched with the suspicion of Epicureanism. Grotius, too, because of his Socinianism that teaches an identical providence equally common to all religions, did not recognized any particular characteristic truth about it in the book he wrote *On the Truth of the Christian Religion* before the writing of *On the Law of War and Peace*. And when he wrote *On the Law* he did not properly consider a divine providence in agreement with the truth of the Christian religion, which is what instead I believe to have done in the system introduced in the book, if I am not blinded by my personal bias.

AB AEQUANIMO LECTORE PETITIO

[*51*] Tu vero, aequanime lector, scias me in hypocausto, cum lethali praecipitique morbo, tum periculoso et senibus apoplexiam minitante remedio, languentem hoc opusculum lucu-
810 brasse. Deinde, quod viginti ferme abhinc annis libros omnes valere iussi ut in doctrinam de iure naturali gentium aliquid pro mea tenui parte conferrem; pro qua sategi, si in penitissima, multiiuga et varia universi sensus humani bibliotheca me totum abderem, ubi vetustissimos gentium auctores, a quibus vix
815 post mille annos scriptores provenerunt, evolverem. Quod idem sibi faciendum Thomas Obbesius duxit, qui, inter literatos amicos et aequales suos, se, non alia nisi hac via, eius doctrinae principem extitisse et philosophiam hoc ingenti auctario cumulasse gloriabatur; sed satis falso tamen, quia Divinam
820 Providentiam, quae una ipsi tenebricosas rerum humanarum origines perlustranti facem praelucere poterat, meditatus non est, et ita in obscurissima deploratae antiquitatis nocte cum caeco Epicuri casu pererrat, contra cuius doctrinas et principia in primis disputo: quod a me factum dominus Clericus in sua
825 « Bibliotheca » praecipue laudat. Ego in nota ad literam (k), cuius hoc, quod heic dico, caput erat, oblitus sum dicere; erro autem iste sedulo omisit, ne principia indicaret ex quibus qui sunt per ipsum philosophi sua de iure naturali gentium systemata hactenus deducere consueverunt. In quibus est Pufen-
830 dorfius, quem, epicureismi suspicione aspersum, purgari oportuit, Grotius autem, quia socinianismus, quo adtinctus fuit, prave docet Providentiam ita omnibus religionibus aeque promptam ut veritati Christianae religionis, de qua ipsa antea librum scripserat, nihil condat praecipuum; iccirco in libris « De iure
835 belli et pacis » ne cogitavit quidem Providentiam meditari convenienter ad veritatem Christianae religionis; quod nos, nisi nostra plus aequo amamus, in systemate nostro praestitimus.
[*52*] His de caussis et ' sub ' hoc gravi ' exemplo ', si quem heic alium memoriae lapsum offenderis, condonato; si
840 quod autem non ad libellam exactum neve ' ad unguem ' expolitum, aequi ' boni'que c o n s u l i t o .

127

[52] For these reasons and the preceding important example of the serious mentioned skip of mind, if you, O my dear reader, would by any chance stumble on another one, please forgive me. If, in addition, you think that something has not been properly dealt with nor it has been properly polished up on, accept it with an equitable kindness.

Part Three

Dipintura of the *New Science*

The Emblem or Visual Synopsis of the New Science

[See my The Synopsis of the New Science of G. B. Vico
in the Dipintura*]*

On the Life and Character of Giambattista Vico

ON THE LIFE AND CHARACTER OF GIAMBATTISTA VICO[1]

[An Appendix in Benedetto Croce, *The Philosophy of Giambattista Vico*, translated by R.G. Collingwood (Russell & Russell Inc., New York: 1964]

The transformation, half rhetorical, half mythical, which the heat of the national reawakening effected in poets, philosophers, and almost every character of any importance in Italian history, representing them as patriots, liberals, and in open rebellion or secret revolt against the throne and the altar, tried for a time to touch with its magic wand and to work its will upon Giambattista Vico. It was said, among other things, that Vico, conscious of the severe blow dealt by his thought to the traditional beliefs of religion, and warned by his friends, took pains to plunge the New Science into such obscurity that only the finest intellects could perceive its tendencies. But though this legend, energetically spread as it was by the patriots and republicans of 1799, was believed here and there, it could not long stand out against criticism or even against common sense ; and Cataldo Iannelli was right to pass over it with a few words of contemptuous irony.[2]

It is certain from an objective point of view that Vico's doctrines implicitly contained a criticism of Christian transcendence and theology as well as of the history of Christianity. From the subjective point of view it may be that Vico during his youth (of which we know very little) was the victim of religious doubts. Such doubts may have been suggested to

---

[1] Since the preceding portions of this work are strictly confined to the analysis of Vico s philosophy and give no information as to his life and personal character, the reader will not be displeased to find in this appendix a lecture delivered by myself upon the latter subject before the Neapolitan Societá di storia patria on April 14, 1909, and later written down and published in the *Florence Voce* (ist year, No. 43, October 7, 1909). I add for convenience of memory that Vico was born at Naples on June 23, 1668 (not 1670 as he says in his autobiography), and died on January 23 (not 20 as all his biographers say), 1744 : cf. the new edition of the *Autobiografia, carteggio e poesie varie* (Bari, Laterza, 1911), pp. 101, 123, 124.

[2] See for the whole question Croce, *Bibliografia Vichiana*, pp. 9I-95.

him not only by his reading, but by the society of young men of his own age, among whom "libertines," or as contemporary literature still called them "epicureans" or "atheists," were not uncommon[1] In a letter of 1720 to Father Giacchi, he says that at Naples the "weaknesses and errors dating from his early youth" are remembered against him, and that these, fixed in the memory, became as often happens "eternal criteria for the judgment of everything beautiful and complete which he subsequently succeeded in doing." [2]What can these errors and weaknesses have been? Again when the *De universi iuris uno principio et fine uno* appeared, or rather the *Synopsis* which announced its programme "the first voices" which Vico heard raised against him "were tinged with an assumed piety." He found protection and consolation in the face of such criticism in religion itself, that is to say in the approval of Giacchi, "the leading light of the strictest and most holy order of religious."[3] But just as we possess no detailed information as to the criticisms levelled against him on this head, so we have no certain knowledge even of the most general kind as to the religious doubts that may have troubled him. All Vico s writings show the Catholic religion established in his heart, grave, solid and immovable as a pillar of adamant; so solid and so strong that it remained absolutely untouched by the criticism of mythology inaugurated by himself. Nor was Vico an irreproachable Catholic in external demonstration only. He not only submitted every word he ever printed to the double censorship, public and private, of ecclesiastical friends, and led his life as a philosopher and

---

[1] In the Giornali of Confuorto (MSS. in the library of the Neapolitan Historical Soc. xx. c. 22, vol. iii. f. in) under August 1692, we find " certain civil persons were imprisoned in the prisons of St. Dominic by the tribunal of the Holy Office ; among them the doctor Giacinto de Cristofaro, son of the doctor Bernardo ; many others escaped, members of the Epicurean or Atheist sect, who believe the soul to perish with the body." This De Cristofaro is the famous Neapolitan mathematician and jurisconsult, for whom see F. Amodeo, *Vita matematica napoletana*, part iii. (Naples, Giannini, 1905), pp. 31-44; he was Vico's friend. For other notices of the " Epicureans " at Naples at this time see Carducci, *Opere*, vol. ii. pp. 235-6.

[2] Letter of October 12, 1720.

[3] *Ibidem.*

writer among priestly vestments and monastic cowls no less than among legal gowns ; he was even scrupulous enough to desist from his commentary on Grotius, thinking it unseemly that a Catholic should annotate a Protestant writer;[1] and so delicate was his sense of Catholic honor that he refused to admit polemic upon matters of religious feeling. "As to this difficulty" he says to his critics of the *Giornale dei Letterati*, "like that which you propound to me concerning the immortality of the soul, where it appears that you have in hand seven distinct arguments, if they had not been prepared for me by you, I should judge that they go deeper and penetrate to a region which is not only protected and secured by my life and conduct, but which to defend is to outrage. But let us return to our subject."[2] His Catholicism was untainted by the superstition so general and so deeply rooted at the time, especially at Naples, where St. Januarius intervened as an actor and director in every event of public and private life. It was the Catholicism of a lofty soul and mind, not the faith of a charcoal-burner. But Vico never assumed the part of censor of superstitions. He was content with not speaking of them, as one keeps silence concerning the failings of persons or institutions which command one's respect.

II

Vico s attitude towards social and political life resembles in more than one respect his attitude towards religion. There is in him no trace of the missionary, the propagandist, the agitator or the conspirator as there was in some of the Renaissance philosophers, notably Giordano Bruno and Campanella, whom although perhaps because a Neapolitan, Vico never mentions. Certainly, his age and his country were not the time or place for heroes; there was none of that rapid social change and revolution from which heroes spring. Political parties however were

---

[1] Autobiografia, in Opere, ed. Ferrari, 2nd ed. iv. p. 367.

[2] The subject is therefore not the religious objections, which he regarded as a personal insult (Riposta al Giornale dei letterati, in Opp. ii, p. 160.

active in favor of Austria and France, and men were arising who devoted their labors and their lives to one or other of these parties, or were persecuted and fled into exile: and above all this was the period in which culminated the straggle between Church and State, between Naples and Rome, in the person of Pietro Giannone, a man of whom Vico never speaks, just as he never mentions and in fact seems to ignore the entire movement. Political life rolled past over his head, like the sky and its stars, and he never wasted his strength in a vain attempt to reach it. Political and social controversy, like religious, was outside the sphere of his activity. He was indeed a non-political person. We cannot describe it as a fault or a weakness, for everyone has his limitations; one struggle excludes another, and one labor makes others impossible. Not that he avoided all contact with political life and its representatives. Only too often he was compelled to pay his respects to both, in the form of histories, speeches, verses and epigrams in Latin and Italian ; and these alone would be sufficient material for the reconstruction of Neapolitan history in all its vicissitudes from the end of the seventeenth century to the middle of the eighteenth : the Spanish vice regency, the conspiracy and revolution attempted by the partisans of Austria, the reaction and re-establishment of the Spanish vice regency, the Austrian conquest, the Austrian vice regency, the Spanish re-conquest and the reign of Charles Bourbon. But Vico, "very pliant because of his necessity"[1] and as professor of eloquence in the royal university, was compelled to supply the literary compositions required by the solemnities of the day, just as the draper supplied hangings and the plasterer volutes and arabesques. And what hangings and arabesques he produced ! The Spanish style of the seventeenth century was still predominant in literature ; and this fact isalone almost enough to explain the extravagance and ornateness, as it seems to us, of Vico s flood of panegyrics. The indifference and innocence of his own attitude may be illustrated by the passage in his autobiography where after mentioning the Panegyricus Philippo V

---

[1] Opp. vi. p. 20

inscriptus composed by himself to the order of the Spanish viceroy, the Duke of Ascalona, he goes on as if it was a mere nothing, with no connexion but a simple "soon after": "soon after, this kingdom having passed under the rule of Austria, the lord Count Wirrigo of Daun, at that time governor of the imperial armies in this country, ordered me" to compose inscriptions for the expiatory monuments to Giuseppe Capece and Carlo di Sangro,[1] the two rebels against Philip V. executed by the previous government some years before in the suppression of the conspiracy of Macchia described by Vico from the Bourbon point of view in his De Parthenopea coniuratione. But this implies no baseness of character on Vico s part. It must be said that in these writings of his, orator and panegyrist though he is, he can never be called a flatterer. The flatterer, the man without a conscience, reviles and calumniates the enemies of the man he is praising, or even strikes the conquered : and this is servility. But Vico, who though he knew who the Italian or Neapolitan was that sent to the *Acta Lipsiensia* the note injurious to himself, and might easily have ruined him, since the note was anti-Catholic in tendency, generously refused to reveal his name,[2] gave no doubt his services as professor of eloquence but refrained from trafficking in the interests of the patrons whom he praised. Of the Life of Antonio Carafa which he composed for a com mission and married one of his daughters on the proceeds, he says that the work was "tempered by honor towards the subject, reverence towards princes and the just claims of truth."[3] And to return to the case of Capece and Sangro mentioned above, when he spoke in the *De Parthenopea coniuratione* of the death of these two enemies to the triumphant party, he shows here too in various details the nobility of his spirit: of Capece, who refused to surrender to the Spanish soldiers, he writes "exposing his breast to death, and demanding death with his warlike arms, he fell unrepentant, a most valiant manner of death, were it only honored in its cause"

---

[1] Vico, *Autobiography*, in Opp. iv, p. 394.
[2] Letter of 4 December 1729, in Opp. VI. p. 32.
[3] Autobiography, in Opp. IV, pp. 366.

(ostentans pectus neci eamque infensis armis efflagitans, inexoratus occubuit, fortissimum mortis genus si causa cohonestasset). Of Sangro too, having reported the rumour that Louis XIV sent him a reprieve which arrived too late, he adds "whence the condemned man, who had already suffered the penalty, is the more to be pitied (unde maior damnati qui iam poenas persolverat, miseratio)[1]. He must have known, and doubtless did know, that most of the persons whose praises he composed were of very little worth. To read his panegyrics, one would suppose that Naples was adorned with a nobility resplendent in its virtue, cultivation and learning : and yet, in giving Father De Vitry the information he desired upon the condition of studies in Naples, Vico did not conceal the facts: "the nobles slumber amid the enjoyments of a life of pleasure." [2] His pupil Antonio Genovesi has preserved to us one of his satirical expressions upon this nobility, often in extreme poverty but always proud and ready to go hungry at home in order to drive abroad in coaches sumptuously dressed.[3] With reference to the literary duke of Laurenzano, he formulated the theory that "noble" writers could not fail of excellence:[4] and yet I have discovered among his papers the manuscript of a book by this duke, rewritten from end to end by the same Vico.[5] Such are the contradictions and the transactions into which a poor man falls when the pressure of want has made him timid and cautious ; so that it is not easy to determine how far his admiration was merely assumed at command or by complaisance, or how far his feeling of social inferiority developed into a real admiration for those above him in the scale, who possessed riches and dignity and everything he lacked and were the "seigneurs."

---

[1] Opp. I. pp. 367-368
[2] Opp. VI. p. 9
[3] He said that many of them "dragged their carriages with their own guts" (Suppl. alla BibL vich. p. 10).
[4] Opp. vi. p. 95.
[5] Bibl. Vich. pp. 27-28.

III

For, as is well known, his financial state was always of the gloomiest. The son of a small Neapolitan bookseller, he was at first compelled to go as a private tutor to a wild town of the Cilento; later, returning to Naples, he tried in vain to obtain the position of secretary of the city, and having in 1699 been elected to the chair of rhetoric, he held that position for thirty-six years at an annual stipend of a hundred ducats. His attempt to pass to a chair of greater importance in 1723 failed, whether owing to ill-luck or to inability he recognised that he was a "man of little spirit in matters of utility,"[1] he was compelled to give up hopes of academic advancement. He was therefore obliged to eke out his resources by literary work such as we have mentioned, and still more by private lessons ; he not only kept school at his own house as well as at the university, but he went up and down other men s steps to teach grammar to youths or even to children. His family life was not a happy one. His wife was illiterate, and had not the qualities with which her sex sometimes compensates the defect; she was incapable of any domestic employment whatever, so that her husband had to take her place. Of his children, one girl died after a long illness and the heavy expenses which embitter the diseases of the poor one boy showed such strong vicious tendencies that the father was compelled to seek the intervention of the police and place him in a house of correction. So sublimely irrational was his fatherly affection that upon this occasion when he saw from the window the police officers he had called in, coming to take his miserable and beloved son away, he ran to him crying, "my son, flee!"[2] He was indeed of an extremely affectionate disposition; a fact which may be gathered for instance from the noble and touching speech he composed on the death of his friend Donna Angela Cimini, from the tone of pity and indignation with which in the *Scienza Nuova* he spoke of the

---

[1] Autobiography in Opp. IV. p. 349
[2] Villarosa in the additions to the Autobiography (Opp. iv. p. 420).

oppressed plebeians whose history he is investigating or of the tragic figures of Priam and Polyxena, the romance of which he feels keenly; and finally, from certain stylistic details scattered here and there, such as the aphorism (no. xl.) where he says that witches in order to solemnise their rites "slay without pity and cut in pieces most lovely and innocent children," quite upset, in the most inopportune but significant fashion, by the fate of these little persons, whom his excited imagination adorns with a superlative loveliness. His greatest domestic happiness came from his daughter Luisa, a cultured and poetical soul, and his son Gennaro, who shared with him and ultimately succeeded to his chair. When, in his panegyric on the Countess of Althann, he calls ironically upon the philosophers who dispute as they walk in pleasant gardens or beneath painted porticoes, free from the agony and weariness of "wives in travail" and "children wasting away with disease,"[1] we feel that he is speaking from his own experience and smarting under the memory of domestic troubles. We often meet, especially in these days, with men of some talent who consider themselves freed from this or that humble duty : and we ought the more to admire this man of genius who on the contrary accepted them every one, and (to use a phrase of Flaubert s) while thinking the thought of a demigod lived the life of a townsman or even that of a man of the people. He had acquired the habit of reading, writing, thinking and composing his works while discussing matters with his friends amid the uproar of his children."[2]

His health was never very good : his friends called him "Mastro Tisicuzzo"[3]: very weak in youth, he was in his old age afflicted with ulcers in the throat and pains in his thighs and legs. In a word, the repose, the peace, the tranquillity which other philosophers enjoy all their life or for long periods together was always lacking to Vico. He was forced to play both Martha and Mary, working at every moment for his own and his family s practical needs and working at the same time to

---

[1] Opp. VI. p. 235.
[2] Autobiography in Opp. IV, p. 366.
[3] "Mr. Skin-and-bones," cfr. *Bibliografia Vichiana*, p. 87.

fulfil the mission to which he was devoted from his birth and to give concrete form to the spiritual world that moved within him.

IV

Thus we need not invent or demand a heroic Vico, looking for him in the life of religion, society or politics. The true hero is the Vico who stands before us, the hero of the philosophic life. Others beside ourselves have noticed his love for the word "hero" and all its derivatives," heroism," ""heroic" and so on: and the continual use and varied application he makes of it. Heroism was for him the mighty virgin force which appears in the beginning and reappears in the reflux of history. This force he must surely have felt in himself as he labored for the truth and, overthrowing obstacles of every kind, opened up new paths of science. It was this force that enabled him to overcome the youthful uncertainties, fears and defeats which sometimes plunged him in a profound individual and cosmic pessimism, visible in the poem entitled "Feelings of One in Despair" to rise to the certainty of scientific method enunciated in the *De nostri temporis studiorum ratione* and his first attempt at philosophico-historical research repre sented by the *De antiquissima Italorum sapientia* ; and from this point, abandoning in part his own thought and weaving a new tissue of what remained, led him to the De uno universi iuris principio et fine uno and to the Scienza Nuova "after twenty five years, as he says of the discoveries contained in that work, "of unremitting and toilsome thought." The work completed by this poor teacher of grammar and rhetoric, by this pedagogue whom a contemporary satirist saw "lean, with a rolling eye, ferule in hand," by this unhappy paterfamilias, is amazing and almost terrifying ; such is the mass of mental power compressed into it. It is a work at once reactionary and revolutionary : reactionary in relation to the present, by its attachment to the traditions of the ancient world and the Renaissance ; revolutionary as against the present and the past in laying the foundations of that future later to be known as the Nineteenth century.

Within the domain of science, this humble man of the people became an aristocrat : and the "lordly style"[1] which he falsely ascribed to the wretched writings of the proud nobles and pompous prelates of his day was in reality his own. He loathed the polite and social literature which was gradually spreading in France and Italy and other European countries, the "ladies books."[2] But he avoided no less that other class of treatise which we nowadays call handbooks, which explain in detail elementary definitions and facts ascertained by others ; books useless except to the young.[3] Vico, who suffered quite enough from the young within the circle of his school, saw no need to sacrifice to them any part of his own inviolable life of science. The public towards which he looked was not composed of boys, lords and ladies. When he wrote, his first practical thought was, "what would a Plato, a Varro or a Quintus Mucius Scaevola think of the fruits of his thought?" and secondly, "what will posterity think?"[4] Among his contemporaries he looked only at the republic of letters, the brotherhood of scholars, the Academies of Europe a public which did not require him to repeat what had been already discovered and stated in the course of the history of science, and was perfectly familiar to him, but only demanded the exposition of such thoughts as constituted a real advance of knowledge : not voluminous works, but "little books, all full of original things."[5]

His public was an ideal one, which sometimes in his simplicity he confused with the actual professional scholars and the critics of literary reviews : and the mistake often caused him surprise. Short books on metaphysical subjects seemed to him to have a peculiar power, as in fact they have ; he compares them very justly with religious meditations "which briefly set forth a small number of points"; and are more valuable for the development of the Christian spirit than "the most eloquent and

---

[1] Bill. vich. p. 82. 2 Opp. vi. p. 93.
[2] Ibid. vi. p. 5.
[3] Ibid. ii. p. 123
[4] Ibid. v. p. 50 (note)
[5] Ibid. ii. p. 148.

lucid sermons of the most gifted preachers."[1] This love of brevity inspires his refusal to burden with many books the republic of letters, which, he says, is already sinking beneath the weight. He left his discourses unpublished, only printed his De ratione out of a sense of duty, and often expressed a desire that the Scienza Nuova alone should survive him, as the work which summed up in itself the concentrated and perfected fruits of all hisearlier efforts.

His aristocratic ideal was accompanied by the loftiest dignity and the profoundest loyalty in his conception of the life of science. From his polemics we might compile a whole catechism on the right method of conducting literary con troversy. We must aim at victory, he says, not in the controversy but in the truth ; hence he desires that it should beconducted "in the calmest manner of reasoning," because "he who is strong does not threaten, and he who is right does not use insults the dispute must at any rate be interspersed with peaceful words "showing that the minds of the disputants are placid and tranquil, not excited and perturbed." To opponents whose objections are vague he replies, "the judgment is in too general terms : and serious men never deign to reply except to particular and determinate criticisms made upon them." When these same opponents appeal to the "refined taste of the age, which has banished," etc., etc., he replies contemptuously, a grave criticism this, in truth: it is no criticism at all. In thus taking refuge from one's opponents before the tribunal of one's own judgment, by saying that what they say is a thing of which one has no idea, from an opponent one becomes the judge. He refused to rely upon his authorities, but yet did not undervalue them ; authority ought to "make us attentive to seek the causes which could have induced authors, especially the most weighty, to adopt such and such opinions." Again, accused of attributing errors to philosophers so as to be able to refute them with ease, like Aristotle, he protests with dignity: "I would rather enjoy my own small and simple

---

[1] For instance in his letter to Saliani, November 18, 1725, published in Bibl. vich. pp. 97-8, the autograph being in my possession.

stock of knowledge than be compared in bad faith with a great philosopher." His moderation may be illustrated by his splendid eulogy of Descartes, though he spent the best part of his mental powers in opposing him. His loyalty is shown by his prompt recognition of his own errors: "I admit/ he says at one point to the critics of the Giornale dei letterati," that "my distinction is faulty."[1] "The reader must not think it ostentatious in us" (he writes in the second Scienza Nuova), that not satisfied with the favourable judgments of such men as these upon our works, we yet disapprove and reject these works. On the contrary, it is a proof of the high veneration and respect in which we hold these men. For rude and haughty writers uphold their works even against the just accusations and reasonable corrections of others : some, who by chance are of a small spirit, sate themselves with the favourable judgments they receive and because of these go no further towards perfection : but in our case the praise of great minds has increased our courage to amend, to complete, and even to recast in a better form this work of ours."[2]

His scientific life was upright, worthy of a serious searcher after truth; his emotional life disturbed and restless, worthy of one who sees face to face the truth he has long sought and desired, and rejoices in the power of laying it before mankind. Hence his lofty poetry, expressed not in verse but in prose, and especially in the Scienza Nuova. "Vico is a poet," writes Tommaseo : "he brings fire from smoke, and lively images from metaphysical abstractions : he reasons as he narrates and depicts while he reasons : over the mountain-tops of thought he does not walk, he flies ; and in one sentence he often compresses more lyrical feeling than may be found in many an ode."[3] De Sanctis saw in the Scienza Nuova the progress of a poem, almost a new Divina commedia. Sublime

---

[1] 1 See the Riposte in Opp. ii. passim.

[2] 2 Opp. v. p. 10.

[3] 3 G. B. Vico e il suo secolo in the volume La Storia civile nella letteratura (Turin, Loescher, 1872), p. 104 : cf. a judgment on Vico as a writer, ibid. pp. 9-10.

like Dante, he was more severe than Dante himself; if the lips of the Ghibelline show at times the flicker of "a passing smile," Vico looks at history with a face "that never smiles." Moreover, the man whose style has been so often criticised is not a commonplace writer ; he was as careful a student of pure Tuscan[1] as he was a fine connoisseur, according to Capasso, of Latin phraseology.[2] But he was faulty in the arrangement of his books, because his mind did not master all the philosophical and historical material it had accumulated ; he wrote carelessly because wildly and as if possessed by a demon : and hence arise the lack of proportion and the confusion in the various parts of his work, within single pages and single paragraphs. He often gives the impression of a bottle of water quickly inverted, in which the liquid trying to issue forth so presses against the narrow opening "that it comes out painfully, drop by drop." Painfully, by fragments, and disjointedly. One idea while he is expressing it recalls another, that a fact, and that another fact : he tries to say everything at once, and parenthesis branches off into parenthesis in a manner to make one s brain reel. But these chaotic periods, weighted as they are with original thoughts, are no less woven of striking phrases, statuesque words, phrases full of emotion, and picturesque images. A bad writer, if you will, but his is the kind of bad writing of which only great writers possess the secret.

V

The philosophical heroism of Vico asserts itself not only in the internal struggle with himself for the elaboration of his science. It was exposed to other and sterner trials. The position reached by his thought, opposed as it was to the present, and while apparently reactionary turned in reality towards the future, inevitably prevented him from being under stood. No doubt this is the fate of every man of genius : his inmost

---

[1] Opp. iv. pp. 333-4 ; vi. pp. 41, 140.
[2] Bibl. vich. p. 87.

thought is never understood, even when social fortune seems to favour him, even when he arouses enthusiasm and finds a host of disciples and imitators. The words which Hegel is said to have uttered on his deathbed "one only of my pupils understood me, and he misunderstood me" admirably express this historical necessity : the man whom his age fully understands dies with his age. And yet the dis proportion between the value of a man s thought and his contemporaries failure to understand it has seldom if ever been greater than in Vico s case. If he had been free from other causes of discontent, this alone would have been sufficient.

The "desire for praise," which in other than commonplace minds is a desire to see what they think true and good shared, approved and universalised among other minds, was always with him a "vain desire." He was the more afflicted by this misunderstanding and indifference because, as we may well suppose, he was fully conscious of the importance of his own discoveries. He knew that Providence had entrusted to him a lofty mission : he knew himself to be "born for the glory of his country, and therefore in Italy ; since, being born there and not in Morocco, he became a scholar."[1] When he published the *Scienza Nuova*, he believed that he had fired a mine whose loud explosion he expected every minute. Nothing happened: nobody mentioned it to him so that he wrote some days later, to a friend: "In publishing my work in this city I seem to have launched it upon a desert. I avoid all public places, so as not to meet the persons to whom I have sent it, and if by chance I do meet them, I greet them without stopping ; for when this happens, these people give me not the faintest sign that they have received my book, and so confirm my impression of having published it in a wilderness."[2] He had frankly expected a swift and immediate effect : he had hoped to find, among his contemporaries and acquaintances at Naples, minds ready and intellects open to receive and bear fruit of his thoughts : and he hoped this of monks engaged in composing and

---

[1] 1 Autob. in Opp. iv. p. 385.

[2] 2 Letter to Giacchi, November 25, 1725, in Opp. vi. p. 28.

learning by rote wordy sermons, poetasters rhyming in sonnets and advocates compiling second hand speeches ! Instead of this, he found many sceptical and indifferent, and several inclined to laugh. His *Diritto universale* had been as Metastasio informs ugenerally "blamed for obscurity"; on its publication ; it was not widely read and was hastily criticised for the extravagances which an inattentive and superficial reading revealed at every point.[1] Father Paoli, to whom the author had given a copy, wrote in it a couplet making a joke of its unintelligibility.[2]

The *Scienza Nuova* was in an even worse case. We know that Nicola Capasso, a scholar and well disposed towards Vico, on trying to read it fancied he had lost his wits, and by way of a joke hurried off to his doctor Cirillo, to have his pulse felt.[3] A Neapolitan nobleman when asked by Finetti at Venice what opinion was held of Vico at Naples, said that for a time he had passed for a really learned man, but that later his strange opinions had won him the reputation of an eccentric. "And when he published the Scienza Nuova ?" insisted Finetti. "Oh, by then, replied the other, he was quite mad![4] His detractors even attacked him in the modest profession by which he earned his living; they said he was "good at teaching youths who had completed their course, that is to say when they already knew all they needed," or again, more insidiously, that he was fitted less for teaching than for "giving good advice to he teachers themselves"[5] so that they recognised his superiority only to use it in damaging his private interests.

VI

The indifference of the public and the insincerity or malignity of critics could not for Vico be compensated by the friends and appreciative readers of whom Vico had a certainnumber. How indeed could it have

---

[1] Bibl. vich. p. 40.

[2] Opp. vi. p. 20.

[3] Bibl. vich. p. 26. 6 Ibid. p. 87

[4] Bibl. vich. p. 86 : cf. Autob. in Opp. iv. p. 416.

[5] Autob. in Opp. iv. p. 416.

been otherwise, when he cultivated them artificially with such care and anxiety ?Consider for instance the way in which he cultivated the friendship of Giacchi the Capucin. He praised his "admirable works," his "most divine talents," the "rare sublimity" of his "marvellous and divine ideas." He tells him that he has given to the scholars of the city the eulogistic letter sent to him by Giacchi and that they all admire "the sublime workmanship of the conception" and yet he himself used to rewrite in scholar s Latin the inscriptions Giacchi composed in monk's Latin![1] On another occasion he wrote that the praises of a Giacchi had excited envy and had in certain quarters been described as flatteries. He took no less pains to propitiate the Archbishop of Bari, Muzio di Gaeta, a conceited creature full of his own merits and incapable of speaking except about himself. Muzio wrote a panegyric on Pope Benedict XIII a work of which, though Vico praised it again and again he had never heard enough, and was always covertly or openly demanding new praises. So Vico used to besprinkle him patiently with the desired fluid: "the marvellous work of Your Excellency"; his "lordly diction"; his "Demosthenic digressions"; his eloquence, that philosophic speech employed in Greece by the Academic school, in Rome by Cicero, and "among the Italians by none but Your Excellency!" To the advocate Francesco Solla, who had been his pupil and had subsequently retired into the country, he hinted that the Scienza Nuova looked towards him as one of the few men in the world possessed of a mind penetrating enough to receive it unhampered by any prejudices concerning the origin of mankind.[2] Such were the guileless artifices and the pitiful little schemes by which he contrived to give an illusory satisfaction to his thirst for recognition and praise, and a narcotic to his overwrought nerves. But the final results were miserable enough. Giacchi s letters contain not a word to show that he had ever grasped one of Vico's

---

[1] Published by me in Napoli nobilis, xiii. (1904), f. i., and again in Secondo suppl. alia Bibl. vich. pp. 70-2.
[2] Opp. vi. p. 17.

doctrines or even that he had examined them with any serious interest. Monsignor di Gaeta, after a labyrinth of circumlocutions, admits that he "admired more than he understood" of Vico s works;[1] and possibly he was so much occupied in admiring his own prose that he never read them at all. Solla, in whom Vico placed such hopes, thought the discourse on the death of Angela Cimini superior to all the author s other works, including the Scienza Nuova itself. Vico received a no less incautious compliment from another admirer; though a warm and affectionate one, Esteban.[2] Compliments of a vague and unintelligent kind sometimes reached him in return for the copies of his works which he sent not only to Neapolitan scholars but to those of Rome, Pisa, Padua and even Germany, Holland and England : he sent a copy to Isaac Newton.[3]

Generally, however, these gifts were received in contemptuous silence. At most, Vico acquired the reputation of a scholar among hundreds of scholars, a man of letters among thousands of similar men; a learned man, but nothing more. Among the modest, the insignificant, and the young, Vico no doubt had strong admirers. Among these were the poet, later a sacred orator, Gherardo de Angelis, Solla and Esteban whom we have mentioned, the monk Nicola Concina of Padua, and some more. But though their affection was strong their intelligence was weak. Even Concina admitted while rhapsodising his enthusiasm that he did not very clearly comprehend his master: "Oh, what fruitful and sublime lights are here! If only I had the talent to make use of them, to comprehend their depth and the wonderful art of which I seem to catch a glimpse !"[4] The best service that these friends could do him was to soothe with kindly words Vico s embittered spirit if they could not do so by following his inmost thoughts. This is what Esteban does at the close

---

[1] Ibid. p. no.

[2] Bibl. vich. pp. 103-5.

[3] Opusc., ed. Villarosa, ii. p. 277.

[4] Opp. vi. p. 145.

of the letter in which he excuses himself for his foolish remark on the funeral speech of Angela Cimini in phrases he must have gathered from the master's lips: "Be confident, Sir, that Providence, through channels unimagined by yourself, will cause to spring up for you a perennial fountain of immortal glory!"[1] The Jesuit Father Domenico Lodovico, who wrote the couplet inscribed beneath Vico s portrait, on receiving the *Scienza Nuova* sent to the author with much sound sense a little wine from the cellar and a little bread from the oven of the Jesuit house of the Nunziatella, together with a graceful letter begging the author to accept "these trifles, simple as they are, since the infant Jesus himself did not refuse the rude offerings of pastoral peasants." He suggested too that at the side of the alphabet in the symbolic frontispiece to the work a little dwarf should be added in the posture of one dumb with astonishment like Dante's mountaineer, and that beneath him should be written, "with a significant diaeresis," the name Lodo-vico !️[2] Among the young men of his school there were some who, nourished upon his doctrines, were ready to defend their master with their swords;[3] but we all know the value of these youthful enthusiasms. If these scholars had really assimilated Vico's doctrines or any part of them, we should have found traces of it in the literature or culture of the next generation after Vico ; but such traces are entirely absent. Hardly a single one of his formulae, his historical statements, or conceptions even superficially understood is to be found in Conti at Venice, Concina at Padua, Ignazio Luzan in Spain though the last named was living at Naples when the Scienza Nuova was published;[4] or even, within the author s own neighborhood, in Genovesi or Galiani. Envy, insincerity, gossip, calumny and stupidity provoked violent outbursts of anger on Vico s part. He confesses this fault in his autobiography where he says that he inveighed in too severe a manner

---

[1] Bibl. vich. p. 105.

[2] "I praise Vico" Letter published by me in Bibl. vich. p. 107.

[3] Bibl. vich. pp. 87-8.

[4] Ibid. p. 44.

against the errors of conception or doctrine or the incivility of his literary rivals, when in Christian charity and as a true philosopher he ought to have ignored or pardoned them.[1] But as a matter of fact this fault did not greatly distress him: he thought it rather an ornament. The funeral speech for Angela Cimini contained a kind of hymn to anger, the "heroic wrath which in noble spirits disturbs and shakes to the depths by its boiling all those evil thoughts of the mind, which beget the vile swarm of fraud, deceit and falsehood, and renders the hero frank, truthful and loyal ; and thus making him a partisan of truth, arms him as the valiant knight of reason to do battle with wrong and offence."[2]

Although in his writings he guards "with all his power" against falling into this passion[3] we feel a scarcely repressed torrent of wrath in his private letters whenever he denounces the "miserable pedants who "love learning more than truth," or the common tendency of man to be "all memory and imagination," and so forth. In conversation also, it seems, he could be very violent.

When in 1736 Damiano Romano published a work controverting his theory of the Twelve Tables, Vico, although according to Romano himself he had been spoken of as "most learned" and "most famous," together with other titles of respect," tore the book to pieces with his teeth in a way that made every one present tremble with horror, finding a sign of the deepest malignity in the fact that "a lad like myself should join issue with him."[4] But his outbursts of wrath were succeeded by fits of the deepest dejection. In a sonnet he speaks of himself as over whelmed by that fate "which the unjust hate of others often creates," and says that for this reason he has separated himself from human society to live with himself alone. Some times he shakes off this torpor for a moment: then,

---

[1] Autob. in Opp. iv. p. 416 : cf. the evidence of a pupil in Bibl. vich. p. 89
[2] Opp. vi. p. 254.
[3] Autob. in Opp. iv. p. 416
[4] 3 Bibl. vich. p. 88.

he says: "I draw within myself again, and pressed / By heavy cares, return to where I stood: / My fate and not my fault I do lament. [1]

VII

But among all these troubles, obstacles and disappointments, in the midst of this sadness which often draped his life in black, Vico enjoyed one of the loftiest joys accessible to man; the "life of meditation freed and purified from passion, lived by man in solitude without the turbulent and grievous company of the body": the life of security, because it is "made one with the soul always ready and present which shows man his being rooted in the Eternal that measures all times and walking in the Infinite that comprehends all finite things; it crowns him with an eternal and immeasurable joy not restricted invidiously to certain places nor grudgingly to certain times ; but it can grow up within himself only if without envy of rivalry or fear of diminution it spreads and communicates itself unceasingly to more and more human minds." [2]

That he has attained truth he never doubts, though he never ceases to elaborate it further ; with the system presented in the work on Universal Law, his mind, he says, "rested content." [3] The weariness and even the pain he had suffered were dear to him, because through them he arrived at his discoveries: "I bless the twenty-five full years I have spent in meditation upon this subject, in the midst of the adversities of fortune and the checks I have often received from the unhappy example of great thinkers who have attempted new and weighty discoveries." [4] How could he have done anything but bless these fatigues, pains and adversities, if, whenever he rose above the passionate perturbations of the empirical man and the struggles of the practical man, his mind showed him the inevitable necessity of his toil and of his sufferings, two

---

[1] Sonnet by G. Gentile, // *Figlio di G. B. Vico* (Naples, Pierro, 1905), p. 173
[2] Opp. vi. p. 287.
[3] Ibid. p. 18.
[4] Ibid. pp. 153-4.

necessities fused into one another so as to become one and indivisible? His own philosophical doctrine then brought him the remedy for his ills, and worked in his spirit the catharsis of liberation ; the doctrine of the immanent Providence, or as it was later called, historical necessity, which was his central thought. "Praise be to Providence for ever, which, when the weak sight of mortals sees in it nothing but stern justice, then most of all is at work on a crowning mercy ! For by this task I see that I am clothed upon with a new man ; I feel that everything that goaded me to bewail my hard lot and to denounce the corruption of literature that has caused that lot, has vanished ; for this corruption and this lot have strengthened me and enabled me to perfect my task. And more, it may perhaps not be true, but it would please me, were it true, that this labour has filled me with a .certain spirit of heroism, through which no fear of death any longer disturbs me and my mind feels no disquietude at the words of my rivals. Lastly, it has established me as upon a mighty rock of adamant before the judgment of God, who rewards the work of creation by the approval of the wise, who are always and everywhere few in numbers . . . men of the loftiest intellect, of a learning all their own, generous and great-hearted, whose only labour is to enrich with deathless works the commonwealth of letters."[1] Thus Providence showed him the necessity of all that had befallen or should befall him in his life, taught him resignation and promised him glory.

VIII

So the hot-tempered man became at last tolerant : tolerant with that tolerance, that lofty indulgence which must not be confused with common toleration. The University, in which he had hoped for advancement and towards which he directed the thought of his earlier works, would have none of him; he retired within himself to think out the Scienza Nuova. Now, says he with a smile in which we may still see a trace of bitterness, I owe this work to the University, which, by judging

---

[1] Opp. vi. pp. 29-30.

me unworthy of the chair and not wishing me to be "occupied in treating paragraphs," gave me leisure for meditation: "what greater obligation could I have?"[1]

A friend, Sostegni the Florentine, in a sonnet to Vico, let slip some words in condemnation of the city of Naples for making so little of her distinguished son. Vico in his reply justifies his native place in noble words, as being stern towards him because she expected and desired much of him:

> Stern mother, she caresses not her son,
> Lest so she fall into obscurity,
> But gravely listens, watching as he speaks.[2]

This was the spirit that found expression in the Autobiography, a work which has been misjudged and in fact entirely misunderstood by Ferrari, who censures its prevailing teleological tendency and laments the absence of a "psychological" explanation of Vice's life;[3] as if Vico had not himself explained that he was writing it from a "philosophical" point of view. And what is the meaning of a philosophical treatment of a philosopher s life but an understanding of the objective necessity of his thought and a perception of the scaffolding it involves even where the author at the moment of thinking did not clearly perceive it? Vico "meditates upon the causes, natural and moral, and upon the occasions of his fortunes; he meditates upon the inclinations or aversions he felt from childhood towards this or that branch of study; he meditates upon the opportunities or hindrances which assisted or retarded his progress; he meditates, lastly, upon certain efforts of his own in right directions which bore fruit in the reflections upon which he built his final work, the *Scienza Nuova*, which work was to demonstrate that his literary life was

---

[1] Ibid. p. 29.

[2] Ibid. p. 446.

[3] In the Introduction to vol. iv. of the Opere.

bound to have been what it was and not different.[1] Vico's *Autobiography* is, in a word, the application of the *Scienza Nuova* to the life of its author, the course of his own individual history: and its method is as just and true as it is original. Vico succeeded in part only of his attempt, and could not form a criticism and history of himself to the same extent to which a modern critic and historian is in a position to do whose efforts will again be improved upon by those of the future is too obvious to need emphasizing. The *Autobiography* itself concludes with a blessing upon the author s hardships, a profession of faith in Providence and a sure expectation of fame and glory.

IX

In the last years of his life Vico, enfeebled by age, domestic trouble and illness, "entirely gave up his studies"[2]

> My pen is slipping from my palsied grasp;
> The door of my thought's treasury is closed,[3]

he cries in two mournful lines of a sonnet in 1735. He prepared at this time additions and corrections for a possible reprint of the second *Scienza Nuova*, and incorporated them in the final manuscript of the work; he thought for a time of printing his small work "on the Equilibrium of the Living Body"; (*De aequilibrio corporis animantis*) composed many years earlier and now lost;[4] he still discharged some of the dutiesof his office, such as the speech on the marriage of the king, Charles Bourbon, in 1738. But from 1736 or 1737 his son began to assist him in his professional work, and in January 1741 he was

---

[1] Autob. in Opp. iv. p. 402.

[2] Ibid. 3 Ibid. p. 415.

[3] Opp. vi. p. 425 (Sonnet on the marriage of Raimondo di Sangro, 1735).

[4] Bibl. vich. pp. 38-9.

definitely appointed to the chair on his father's resignation.[1] Vico henceforth lived among his family like an old soldier *exacta militia*, thinking over his past battles and conscious of having done his life's work. His good son read to him for some hours every day out of the Latin classics he had once loved and studied so well. And in this evening of his life he was at least spared the crowning agony suffered in his last years by a philosopher more fortunate than himself, Immanuel Kant; the agony of continuing and completing his system of philosophy, and wearing himself out in a fruitless struggle with thoughts that eluded his grasp and words that no longer obeyed him. Vico had said all he had to say; a great historian of his own life, he knew the moment at which Providence had finished its work in him, closed the door of thought it had so freely opened, and ordered him to lay down his pen.[2]

---

[1] Gentile, // Figlio di G. B. Vico, pp. 30-48.

[2] The documents and the scattered notes used in this lecture and quoted from the contents of my Bibliografia vichiana are now all collected in my edition of the *Autobiografia, carteggio e poesie varie.*

VICO'S SELECTED WORKS

Vico, Giambattista, *The Autobiography*, translated by Max Harold Fisch and Thomas Goddard Bergin, Ithaca, N. Y. Great Seal Books, 1963.

Vico, Giambattista, *The First New Science*, Edited and Translated by Leon Pompa, Cambridge Texts in the History of Political Thought, Cambridge University Press, 2002.

Vico, Giambattista, *On Humanistic Education (Six Inaugural Orations, 1699–1707)*. Ithaca and London: Cornell University Press, 1993.

Vico, Giambattista, *The Art of Rhetoric.* New York-Amsterdam: Rodopi, 1996.

Vico, Giambattista, *Statecraft: The Deeds of Antonio Carafa.* New York and Berlin: Peter Lang Publisher, 2004

Vico, Giambattista, *Universal Right.* Amsterdam & New York: Rodopi, 2000

Vico, Giambattista, Opere: *Varia, il De Mente Heroica e gli Scritti Latini Minori*, Consiglio Nazionale delle Ricerche, vol. 12.

Vico, Giambattista, "A Factual Digression on Human Genius, Sharp, Witty Remarks, and Laughter," in *Forum Italicum*, 2 (1968).

GENERAL BIBLIOGRAPHY

Acampora, G., *Rime scelte di vari poeti napoletani.* Napoli: Printer: Domenico Antonio Parrino, Toleto Street, at the sign of Salvatore, 1702

Armignacco, Teodosio, "Sulle Vici Vindiciae" in *L'edizione critica di Vico: bilanci e prospettive*, ed. Giuseppe Cacciatore, Napoli: Guida Editore, 1997, pp. 167-170.

Capasso, Niccolò. *Varie Poesie di Niccoló Capasso.* Stamperia Simoniana, Napoli, 1761 [with an eulogy of Vico, pp. 27-29].

Colapietra, Raffaele, *Vita pubblica e classi politiche del viceregno napoletano, 1656–1734.* Roma: Edizioni di Storia e Letteratura, 1961.

Colletta, Pietro, *Storia del Reame di Napoli, 1734–1825.* Paris, 1843.

Colletta, Pietro, *History of the Kingdom of Naples 1734–1825.* Translated from the Italian by S. Horner [with a Supplementary Chapter for 1825–1856]. Edinburgh: T. Constable and London: Co. Hamilton, Adams, and Company, 1858.

Costa, Gustavo, "Perche Vico pubblicò un capolavoro incompiuto? Considerazioni in margine a *La Scienza Nuova*, 1730," in *Italica* 82 (2005): 567

Costa, Gustavo, "Vico e l'Inquisizione" in *Nouvelles de la Republique des Lettres* 2 (1999): 93-124.

Croce, Benedetto, *Bibliografia Vichiana.* Accresciuta e Rielaborata da Fausto Nicolini. 2 Vols. Napoli: Riccardo Ricciardi Editore, 1948.

Fabiani, Paolo, *The Philosophy of the Imagination in Vico and*

BIBLIOGRAPHY

Malebranche. Firenze: Firenze University Press, 2009

Giannone, Pietro, *Istoria Civile del Regno di Napoli*. Napoli: Palmyra, 1723.

Giarrizzo, Giuseppe, *Vico, la politica e la storia*. Napoli: Guida Editori, 1981.

Musi, Aurelio & Maria Anna Noto. *Feudalità Laica e Feudalità Ecclesiastica nell'Italia Meridionale*. Palermo: Associazione Mediterranea, 2011.

Naddeo, Barbara Ann. *Vico and Naples: The Urban Origins of Modern Social Theory*. Ithaca and London: Cornell University Press, 2011

Nicolini, Fausto. *La giovinezza di Giambattista Vico* (1668–1700). Bari: Fratelli Laterza, 1932.

Nicolini, Fausto, *Giambattista Vico. Opere*, vol. 4. Laterza, Bari: 1942.

Nicolini, Fausto, *Giambattista Vico. Opere.* Milano: Riccardo Ricciardi Editore, 1953.

Nicolini, Fausto, *Vico Storico*. Napoli: Morano Editore, 1967.

Pinton, Giorgio A., *Horace's Art of Poetry & Vico's Poetic Philosophy*, CreateSpace, 2014.

Pinton, Giorgio A., *Bernardino Martirano: Four Commentaries on Horace's Art of Poetry (Acron, Porphyrio, Parrhasius, Glareanus)*, CreateSpace, 2015.

Ratto, F., *Percorsi della Ricerca Filosofica, Filosofia tra Storia Linguaggio Politica* , Rome: Gangemi Editore, 1990, pp. 29-40.

Ratto, F., "Motivi di una rilettura delle Vici Vindaciae," in *Educação e Filosofia*, XXXIV, 17 (2003), pp. 81-100.

Ruggiero, R., "Le rivendicazioni di Tacito: in margine alle Vici Vindiciae," in *Bollettino del Centro di Studi Vichiani*, XXX (2000), pp. 185-197.

Selden, *De Iure Naturali et Gentium iuxta Disciplinam Hebraeorum*, Argentorati, 1665.

Stone, Harold Samuel, *Vico's Cultural History. The Production and Transmission of Ideas in Naples*, 1685-1750. Leiden: Brill, 1997.

Tommaseo, Niccolò, (1872) "G.B.Vico e il suo secolo." In *Storia Civile nella letteraria*. Firenze: Loescher, 1872, pp. 96–99.

Troyli, Placido, *Istoria generale del reame di Napoli*. Tomo V. Napoli, 1753.

Verene, Donald Phillip, *Giambattista Vico and the New Art of Autobiography: An Essay on the "Life of Giambattista Vico Written by Himself"*, Oxford, Clarendom, 1991.

INDEX OF NAMES

www.ingramcontent.com/pod-product-compliance
Lightning Source LLC
Chambersburg PA
CBHW071357280526
45787CB00001B/365